DREAMS
Your Window to Heaven

DREAMS

Your Window to Heaven

Debbie Johnson

ECKANKAR
Minneapolis

Dreams: Your Window to Heaven

Copyright © 2002 Debbie Johnson

Printed in U.S.A.

Edited by Joan Klemp, Anthony Moore, and Mary Carroll Moore
Author photo by Glamour Shots

Publisher's Cataloging-in-Publication
(Provided by Quality Books, Inc.)

Johnson, Debbie, 1951–
    Dreams : your window to heaven / Debbie Johnson. — 1st ed.,
    p. cm.
    Includes bibliographical references and index.
    LCCN: 2002102471
    ISBN: 1-57043-173-6

    1. Dreams   2. Dreams—Religious aspects.   3. Spiritual life.
I. Title

BF1078.J64 2002   154.6'3
                                       QBI02-200179

Contents

Acknowledgments

My deepest gratitude to Beverly Foster for her incredibly insightful and in-depth editing and editing advice. Thank you for finishing the job you started, even as you entered an exciting new career. Linda Anderson, thank you for your important added comments and for teaching me how important it is to keep taking the next step as a writer. Kimberly Young has my sincere appreciation for her love and support throughout all my projects, and for being the impetus God used to get me started on this one. Thank you to James Davis for his help and support, information and research brain, not to mention his dear friendship.

A special thanks to all of those who contributed dream stories to this book. You are brave and daring Souls who have my greatest esteem.

Sincere and heartfelt appreciation goes to Myron for his love, support, and contributions to this project, including financial support, which is greatly appreciated.

To my dearest friend and spiritual guide, the Mahanta, I give thanks for the miracles and adventures that fill my life, both in the waking and dream state, as well as the inner and outer teachings that are the basis for this book.

Foreword

 $\mathcal{T}$ he ancient Egyptians believed dreams were real experiences. So did the Native Americans, the Aborigines, and other native cultures. Even today many believe that when a person sleeps, Soul leaves the body to experience other worlds.

And what is Soul?

Soul is who you are. You are not your body, which rests while you sleep. You are not your emotions or even your mind. You are Soul, an eternal spark of God, and you experience some level of heaven every time you dream.

Dream books don't usually give you the means to remember and utilize the spiritual aspects of your dream experiences. This one does, because it is based on Eckankar, a world religion that holds dreams in high esteem as a means toward great spiritual experience.

Are you ready for a new level of adventure?

Then let's get started!

1

Exploring the Spiritual World of Dreams

What can dreams do for you? First of all, if you study your dreams you'll find that you have your own connection to Divine Spirit. You don't need someone out here to tell you what is true about your own inner worlds. You should learn how to do it for yourself.

— Harold Klemp, *How the Inner Master Works,* Mahanta Transcripts, Book 12[1]

aula had a recurring dream. She was racing through an airport to catch a plane. Her heart was pounding with anxiety. Would she make it? Frustrated, she missed her plane.

Each time Paula had this dream, she didn't make it to the plane in time. One night the dream was different:

Paula finally made it to the plane in time for her flight. She relaxed in her seat, breathing a sigh of relief. The plane began to take off. Exhilaration filled her whole being. Suddenly, Paula was flying, independent of the plane.

What can dreams do for you? First of all, if you study your dreams you'll find that you have your own connection to Divine Spirit.

1

The feeling of exhilaration and freedom from this dream lasted through Paula's entire day, carrying her on golden wings.

Like Paula's dream experience, your own dreams can bring you some of the greatest adventures you will ever have in this life. Where on earth can you fly without wings, meet loved ones who have died, resolve problems, make decisions easily, and even visit the many levels of heaven?

Throughout history dreams have inspired people to write music, create fabulous art, invent, nurture love, and repair feuds. Dreams have healed the sick and foretold important future events.

A very famous prophetic dream was had by Joseph in the Old Testament. Joseph was able to warn the pharaoh of the coming famine, and Egypt was able to avoid mass starvation.

Julius Caesar received information in dreams about his campaigns to conquer other lands. But when his wife dreamed of his demise and the soothsayer tried to warn him with the now famous statement, "Beware the Ides of March!" Caesar disregarded the warnings and died that day.

Thomas Edison used the twilight time between waking and sleeping to get fresh insights for his inventions. Elias Howe, the inventor of the sewing machine, was able to complete his invention via his dreams.

Descartes, considered the founder of modern philosophy, said the earliest inspiration for his life's work came to him in dreams.

Mozart and Schumann said they first heard their

> Throughout history dreams have inspired people to write music, create fabulous art, invent, nurture love, and repair feuds.

compositions in their dreams. Robert Louis Stevenson said entire stories came to him in dreams.

We may not become famous by keeping close tabs on our dreams, but we can certainly have more fulfilling and very exciting lives. We may even do great things in our own ways. Many people like you and I have solved problems, been more creative, become healthier, and had profound spiritual experiences by working with their dreams. Dreams can take you far beyond the experiences of even the notable and famous, as shown in Paula's flight-of-freedom dream.

Dreams can also make you aware of who you really are: Soul, a divine spark of God. You don't "have" a soul because you *are* Soul. You don't have a higher self, because you are the higher self. Dreams can help you learn to live as this highest self, your highest viewpoint of life. And from that viewpoint, you can do just about anything!

Interpreting your dreams may actually introduce you to your spiritual destiny in this life. After all, God is speaking to you in your dreams. Actually God is speaking to us all the time, but when we're dreaming, we are often more open to God's voice. You have your own personal connection with God. Why not strengthen it through your dreams?

In dreams you may talk with loved ones who have died, helping you to heal the grief. You may meet your spiritual guide, angel, or dream master. You can learn who you really are as a divine being. If spiritual awareness is important to you, you'll find a wonderful avenue of new spiritual doorways and windows in your dreams. It will be up to you to open them.

Dreams can also make you aware of who you really are: Soul, a divine spark of God.

If you've ever had a fear of death, working with your dreams can help you visit the many levels of heaven and explore them while still living on earth. When you pay attention to your dreams, you may find you're prepared for the changes that life always brings.

In the following pages I'll share with you how dreams helped me make it through the loneliest of times, recognize the man who was to be my husband, make life-changing decisions, solve problems in my writing career, and resolve financial concerns. You'll also discover how many others have had a smoother ride on life's bumpy highway by working with their dreams. Specific techniques will be given to help you in your dream explorations.

WHAT ARE DREAMS?

Some people think dreams are the result of eating too much pizza late at night! Others, like Freud, would say dreams are a call from the unconscious, revealing your hidden desires. One expert on dreams, Harold Klemp, says that dreams are real experiences in the many levels of heaven. I, too, believe that dreams are real experiences. I've proven this to myself by studying and working with my dreams. You can prove this to yourself as well by using the dream exercises throughout this book.

Soul is in a physical body to learn while we are in this school called earth. God is constantly teaching us in this school, and our dreams are a higher form of education!

In our waking lives we're trying desperately to understand life and why certain things happen to us.

Life is teaching us the lessons we need, as fast as we're able to learn them. However, we can only take in so much of life's lessons at a time. Fortunately, the symbolic nature of dreams allows us to decode life's message in our own time and our own way.

There are many views on dreams and their meanings, at least one for every different culture on earth. From spiritual to psychological significance, dreams have been dissected throughout history, yet they still remain a mystery to many.

All these views are valid in their own way. But there's one religion that takes dream study to a new spiritual level, giving dream work more clarity, understanding, and dynamic success. That religion is Eckankar, Religion of the Light and Sound of God. Eckankar's spiritual leader, Harold Klemp, is regarded as an expert on the spiritual nature of dreams. He's written many books that include dream experiences and information; some of these books are referenced in these pages.

> The realm of dreams will take you far beyond your daily life into levels of love and awareness that you have only dreamed possible.

Having studied, explored, and worked with the dream teachings of Eckankar for almost thirty years, I've found they provide a level of understanding and insight unsurpassed in any dream book or study available today. The best part is they are simple and effective, as truth usually is. This book is based upon those teachings.

A rich dessert of many layers, the realm of dreams will take you far beyond your daily life into levels of love and awareness that you have only dreamed possible.

What Do You Want from Your Dreams?

The first logical step in dream study is to clarify your goals. If you know exactly where you're headed, it's much easier to get there! This first technique will lay the foundation for your future dream adventures.

Dream Technique: Clarifying Your Goals

1. Grab a blank notebook, or staple a stack of scratch paper together until you can get a notebook. This will be the basic multipurpose tool you can use to record, remember, interpret, and review your dreams. Later in this chapter you'll be given details about keeping a dream journal.

2. Ask yourself the simple question What do I want from my dreams? Write the question and, underneath it, write your answer. Leave room to jot down more notes later as you think about things to add.

3. Rewrite these goals anytime your interest level changes.

Ask yourself the simple question What do I want from my dreams?

What Good Can We Get from Our Dreams?

I had the following dream:

My husband was driving up to me in our car. The car was packed with all of our belongings. I knew we were moving and even where.

I woke up with a start and said, "Oh, no! We're moving." My husband said, "Yes, I know, I've been thinking about it too." When I told him what I had dreamed and where we were moving he said, "I've known for a while and even tried to tell you, but you didn't seem to want to hear it."

My dream helped me accept something I would not have accepted in the waking state, as I never intended to leave that area.

Then when we were about to move, I became very sad. I didn't want to leave. We were living in a city I loved and where I had very dear friends. I felt secure, snuggled in love and warmth for the first time in my life. Now we were leaving.

I woke up in the middle of the night feeling panic and anxiety. What was causing such turmoil? Then I remembered that it was probably the move and tried to settle back down to sleep. I dreamed that:

We were preparing to move to our new location along with many other people being asked to leave the city. I was very sad. I left some plastic jewelry for a woman with a small child who was staying behind.

I'd been spending time with an old friend, with whom I had a close bond. He exuded a sweetness, like he had blossomed into a spiritual being.

I was sad to leave all my friends there, so I cried as I packed.

When I awoke, I had a song in my head, "Nothing's Gonna Stop Us Now." I wrote down the dream and the title of the song. Then I took a good look at what it all might mean to me. The woman and little girl

When I awoke, I had a song in my head, "Nothing's Gonna Stop Us Now." I wrote down the dream and the title of the song.

were me and my mother. It was time to leave the past behind. The gift of plastic jewelry was telling me that I need not give much to my past, if anything, but a token of gratitude for the lessons learned.

The symbol of my friend represented the bonds of friendship in that city that were wonderful and uplifting in many ways, but it was time to move on to even more uplifting experiences.

The song told me that I was letting go of the past! I had somehow worked out the panic and anxiety in my dreams, and I was getting ready to move—and keep moving—on to a whole new experience! Perhaps it would be even better than the last. The move was important, and my spiritual life has improved in many ways since then. I'm sure the best is yet to come, as always, and I keep paying attention to my dreams.

To take advantage of all the information, awareness, and healing dreams can bring, first we must remember them!

How Can You Remember Your Dreams?

The scientific study of dreams did not begin until the mid–twentieth century with American scientists Nathaniel Kleitman and Eugene Aserinsky.[2] They awakened sleep-study subjects when brain-wave activity reached certain rhythms and found they had been dreaming. Others noticed that at the time of this heightened brain-wave activity, the subjects' eyes were moving back and forth very rapidly under their eyelids. This was later termed rapid eye movement, or REM, sleep.

This phenomenon has been found in humans and animals, and now even in fetuses.

REM sleep is so necessary that without it, people become anxious and irritable. This has been proven in certain studies. When our eyes are moving very quickly during sleep, we are likely dreaming. You may want to test this yourself with a partner. Agree to a wake-up call or nudge when the other person's eyes are moving rapidly. Was there a dream going on?

You can use any of several techniques given in this chapter to better remember your dreams.

To prove to yourself that you do dream, start by remembering more. You can use any of several techniques given in this chapter to better remember your dreams. Give yourself at least thirty days to make a dream technique work.

According to *Teach Yourself to Dream,* by Dr. David Fontana,[3] you can remember your dreams by focusing attention on them, believing they have special meaning to you, and taking time to look for that meaning. People in many cultures do this automatically because they believe that dreams are an incredibly important part of their lives.

The intent to remember and moving forward with the assumption that you *will* remember actually helps you remember. Give yourself time for this. Belief is the most powerful tool of all, as many successful people have proven. Walt Disney was a perfect example with his "Imagineers" and his unbounded enthusiasm for his goals. He never gave up, even in the face of financial ruin. If you can have this kind of belief in yourself, you can do anything. Then remembering your dreams will be easy!

When you first begin to write down your dreams, you may have just a trickle of remembrance. The way to remember more is to always write something in your dream journal, even if it only is "I remember . . ." and nothing else! Be sure to write any phrase, image, or word that comes to mind.

I've interpreted whole dreams from writing just one word. For example, the word *man* instilled a feeling of fear for me. Images followed the feeling, such as a man moving toward me menacingly. I then connected this image with something going on in my life at the time, a misguided loyalty to a failing relationship.

> The important part is the feeling that goes with the dream.

The important part is the feeling that goes with the dream. Sometimes I write a word, then a feeling comes along after it. Often more words and images come too. I call this phenomenon a string of pearls, because each word or feeling is like a pearl on a strand. If I can pull up one, other pearls of wisdom in the form of words, images, or feelings may follow. Also, just beginning the process of writing—making the motion—will prime the pump, if you will, to get your subconscious to begin to help you remember your dreams.

An easy method people have found for remembering their dreams is to keep their dream journal by the bed. Some people have a flashlight next to it to use when they record late-night dreams. I used to have a handheld tape recorder so I didn't need to turn on a light. Another trick is to tape a small narrow flashlight to a pen. The following is an exercise to help you use your journal to remember.

Dream Technique: For Remembering

1. Belief—Before you go to sleep, tell yourself you will remember your dreams as soon as you pick up the pen or pencil to write them down in the morning.

2. Action—Every morning for thirty days, as soon as you awaken, pick up the pen or pencil and write anything you can remember, even if it's only one word like *dog, orange, man,* or *fear.* If you don't remember anything, just begin writing immediately, "I remember, I remember, I remember" until you remember something or have written this fifteen times. Then let it go until the next time you wake up.

Before you go to sleep, tell yourself you will remember your dreams as soon as you pick up the pen or pencil to write them down in the morning.

Believe it or not, the simple technique above is one of the best ways to remember your dreams. Here are some other fun remembering ideas.

TIPS TO HELP YOU REMEMBER DREAMS

1. Go to bed early. Getting a good night's rest is helpful to clearing your mind and gives you a greater opportunity for dreams.

2. Suggest to yourself in words either spoken or written, "I will remember my dreams when I wake up."

3. When you awaken, don't move! Keep your eyes closed. Lie as still as you can as your dream

images filter in. Ask yourself, What dream is here? Once your body regains total wakefulness, dreams fade quickly.

4. When you get a sense of an image or a part of the dream, it's often the end of the dream. Ask yourself what happened just before that image instead of trying to jump right to the beginning of the dream. You may find it easier to piece together.

5. If you are excited about remembering your dreams and want a trigger, try setting an alarm to wake you in the middle of the night. It may only take a few days to learn to awaken on your own after a dream.

6. If you have a mate, ask him or her to watch you when you sleep for signs of REM, or rapid eye movement. Request they wake you when they see your eyelids fluttering. You will likely recall your dream immediately.

7. Try one of the above techniques for thirty days.

8. Do any of the other exercises in this book that speak to your heart. The more you work with your dreams, the more you will remember them. Just putting your attention on your dreams, consistently, will bring results.

The following is a technique that takes some discipline but will help you develop your ability to remember.

Dream Technique:
Waking Technique for Remembering

This technique improves your memory of events, whether awake or in the dream state, even though the technique itself uses the waking state as a platform for the exercise.

Just as you close your eyes in bed, recount the day's events, going backward. Start with what happened just before you went to bed, and trace backward to the time you got up that morning.

As you become proficient at this, you will find yourself remembering your dream events more clearly as well.

Adapted from a spiritual exercise by Harold Klemp

A firm commitment to working with your dreams will also further your success with any technique in this book.

KEEPING A DREAM JOURNAL

One important technique for remembering dreams is a long-term commitment. A firm commitment to working with your dreams will also further your success with any technique in this book. That commitment can be as simple as keeping a dream journal handy at your bedside and writing down whatever comes to mind when you wake up. Whenever you travel, take your journal with you.

Keeping a dream journal can also make your life easier to understand. Everyday challenges can be resolved more readily through working with your dreams. This book will give you many ways to use your journal, and you'll begin to see miracles in the tapestry of your day-to-day life.

IF YOU ARE NOT CONVINCED BY NOW

If you've never kept a dream journal and you're seriously seeking answers in your dreams, a dream journal is almost as necessary as a hammer is to drive a nail. You can be creative and use other methods, but the journal will help you see the patterns in how you work best with your dreams.

A writer who has several books published still finds his dream journal to be the best inspiration for both his professional and his personal life. He says that his dream journal is where he learns, as he's writing in it. He reviews his journal every day; it inspires him and helps him through rough times.

The people I respect most in my life are dedicated to their dream journals. There's something special in the writing process that brings about results. It's a very intimate communication between your outer life and yourself as Soul. It can also be a form of communication between you and God. The journal will not judge you, criticize you, or interrupt you! Its healing power is magical.

YOU CAN TAKE IT A STEP AT A TIME

Recording your dreams is something that can develop slowly and naturally over time. If you are just beginning, you may want to follow the advice of Harold Klemp from his book *The Spiritual Exercises of ECK*. He writes that you can begin your dream study with a nap. Set an alarm for twenty minutes and, when you wake, write whatever you remember from your dream.

Harold Klemp says the first rule for a dream

> If you've never kept a dream journal and you're seriously seeking answers in your dreams, a dream journal is almost as necessary as a hammer is to drive a nail.

journal is to write simply. It's easier and quicker to get the dream down on paper.

The sample from a dream journal that follows will give you a goal to shoot for over the next several months to a year. You don't have to begin using all the pieces at once. Take it a step at a time.

TAKE FULL ADVANTAGE OF YOUR JOURNAL

You can use your dream journal for anything you want. Eventually you may include some things that will be covered in later chapters—such as waking dreams, waking experiences that relate to present challenges, realizations, or insights from contemplation. It could also become your own personal method of prayer or inner connection with God. When you have questions in your life and you need answers, you can often see a pattern of truths in your day-to-day life by looking through your journal. It is rich with your insights, dreams, and experiences.

Just to help you get started, here's a sample taken from entries in my own dream journal. You can use it as a launching pad. Keep your journal entries simple to begin with, and enjoy yourself!

When you have questions in your life and you need answers, you can often see a pattern of truths in your day-to-day life by looking through your journal.

SAMPLE DREAM-JOURNAL PAGES

1/10/_ _ (month/day/year)
DREAM (during a lonely time in my life)

I was in a house with several people who were staying there together. I met my new in-laws, and we were all sleeping together in the same room.

I remember feeling very secure.

I remember thinking, These people feel like family.

Interpretation: We were staying together as a family, and I feel as if I know these people. Perhaps this is a sort of prophetic dream (I am still single). I woke up feeling very secure and well loved. I wonder if this means I will be meeting my mate soon? Or could it mean I am always surrounded by love? My spiritual family is always around me. I feel loved; that's the most important part to me.

I wonder if this means I will be meeting my mate soon? Or could it mean I am always surrounded by love?

2/5/_ _

WAKING DREAM

I saw a sign in a window that said, "Marriage is still in style!" Then I saw two doves flying by as I was wondering if that meant me too.

Interpretation: Perhaps I will get married again.

3/6/_ _

SPIRITUAL EXPERIENCE IN DREAM

There was a feeling of such great love. Like I would never be alone. I would always have love.

Interpretation: I know now that there will always be love in my life and probably marriage at some time in the near future.

3/15/_ _

PAST-LIFE AWARENESS IN DREAM

Someone stabbed me in the back and said, "You will never marry my sister as long as I live!" In the dream I turned around and killed him. I married his sister but could never get over the fact that I had murdered him.

Interpretation: Now I see that I probably have a little more past-life karma (lessons) to work out before I'm ready to get married again.

3/18/_ _
LETTERS
Dear God,

Do I need to work something out with that past life in order to be free to marry again this lifetime?

Dear Dream Master,

Please give me a dream that will help me know the next step to take in working with my blocks to meeting the right mate.

These dream-journal entries helped me see the steps I was taking and needed to take in order to fulfill my dream of marriage to a mate who is right for me.

Keeping my journals has helped me make sense of a life that could otherwise look chaotic. It keeps me viewing my life as a game and a challenge rather than an effort. Life is more fun when I can view it with a light heart, as I would while working a puzzle. My journal helps me keep a relaxed viewpoint, making me feel as though I'm playing detective, looking for clues to solve the mystery of life.

> Keeping my journals has helped me make sense of a life that could otherwise look chaotic.

TO KEEP TRACK OF DREAMS, KEEP AN INDEX

Inside the front cover of each journal, you can also log your dreams by category and date. This helps me track patterns so I can run my life more smoothly.

SAMPLE DREAM INDEX

Dream Categories	Dates of Entries (month/day/year)
Career	1/10/_ _ , 3/4/_ _ , 3/12/_ _, 3/15/_ _
Creative / artistic pursuits	3/7/_ _
Spiritual unfoldment	2/1/_ _, 10/9/_ _, 10/22/_ _
Continued education	
Primary relationship	3/12/_ _, 4/15/_ _, 6/4/_ _
Children	7/2/_ _, 8/14/_ _
Friendships	
Parents and other family	7/2/_ _
Finances	6/12/_ _, 1/15/_ _
Home/house	
Health	2/10/_ _

You may begin to see a pattern emerging that will help solve some of the riddles of your life.

TO FIND HELP IN YOUR DREAM JOURNAL

When life hands you a new challenge, a decision to make, or a question, try looking in your dream log under the appropriate topic. Look up all related dreams or entries on the dates listed under that topic.

You may begin to see a pattern emerging that will help solve some of the riddles of your life. In general, it's a good idea to review your dream journal regularly, perhaps monthly, for an overview of your life and your lessons.

Have fun with the process, and make it a game. Your point of view will be more relaxed. You'll see from a higher viewpoint. Specific techniques to interpret your dreams are in chapter 2, "How to Interpret Your Dreams."

2

How to Interpret Your Dreams

We measure everything here on earth by the waking and sleeping state of the human body. Therefore, we assume that when we go to sleep, we're just starting a dream.

Actually we're tapping into the expanded awareness of Soul as It is existing—as we all are existing—on the inner planes, simultaneously with our existence on the earth. It's a little hard to understand, but Soul is not a two- or three-dimensional being. Soul is multidimensional. It shares all the aspects of God. Soul can be everywhere at all times, and all places at the same time. This is that part of God that you are.

All that remains is to remember at least a little bit of this inner experience. Begin remembering your dreams to get an idea of who and what you are as Soul.

— Harold Klemp, *The Slow Burning Love of God,* Mahanta Transcripts, Book 13[1]

Begin remembering your dreams to get an idea of who and what you are as Soul.

WHY BOTHER INTERPRETING DREAMS?

Was Sasha, the cat, to stay or go? Joel couldn't decide, and his new wife, Donna, was sure the cat herself knew. Donna seriously doubted Sasha was willing to adjust to Joel's two cats. Donna considered finding Sasha a new home before Joel's cats were flown out. Joel felt badly about the whole situation, knowing Donna would miss Sasha, yet Sasha's unusual, ornery behavior seemed to indicate a change was needed.

Fortunately, Joel and Donna knew how to get help in their dreams. So one night just before bed Donna said, "Why don't we ask for an answer tonight?" Joel agreed, and the next morning he woke up with a clear memory of a dream:

Sasha was on the outside of a clear glass door, happy to be outside. Joel was trying to get her to come back in, but she refused. He kept encouraging her to come in, wanting her to feel at home, but she stubbornly resisted.

Joel finally had his answer. The cat wanted to go. She had been trying to tell him in every way she could, and now this dream confirmed it.

Sasha was taken in by one of Donna's friends and was right at home immediately.

What if Joel and Donna hadn't listened to their dreams? The three cats together may have fought and hurt each other, causing untold grief among the humans as well.

This is a small everyday problem, solved through a dream. Many more serious situations have also been resolved via dreams. We can use dreams for

> One night before bed Donna said, "Why don't we ask for an answer tonight?" Joel agreed, and the next morning he woke up with a clear memory of a dream.

every aspect of our lives—from health and diet to love and death, careers to creativity, and education to spiritual awareness. Worries about finances and relationship issues can even be addressed in dreams.

Think of any question or challenge facing you in life, and you can find the tools to resolve it by interpreting your dreams—if you are willing to put in just a little effort and a pinch of time. Believe me, it will save you a bushel of time and effort later on.

When dreams come to us in a way that wakes us up, we can be sure those dreams mean something significant. Interpreting a dream that feels important is important.

WHY DO WE HAVE DREAMS THAT NEED INTERPRETING?

We often have confusing dreams.

Why?

We have what is called a dream censor which blocks the real experience from our conscious mind until it is able to accept the true message. This avoids the shock we might get if we heard the truth all at once. For example, Ginger dreams about a bulldozer and wakes up confused. She hasn't realized yet that she is too pushy and isn't ready to see this truth, so she cannot understand her dream symbol.

Life continues to reveal itself through dreams. When we are ready to see the truth, we're able to interpret our dreams.

Dreams help us get beyond the human experience, back to the awareness of our true self, Soul. As Soul, we understand everything, including how to

Life continues to reveal itself through dreams.

get through our day-to-day trials so we can graduate to the next level. Dreams give us the tools to solve life's mysteries. Interpreting dreams helps us get the messages God is sending us.

> Dreams give us the tools to solve life's mysteries. Interpreting dreams helps us get the messages God is sending us.

We may ask God for help, but perhaps we're only ready for a little bit of the real story. When it becomes more important to us to know what's holding us back in life—and more painful to stay where we are than to move forward—then we may be ready to put the time and effort into interpreting our dreams. It helps to be patient with ourselves until we're prepared to know; then our dreams will be much easier to understand.

LEARNING YOUR OWN DREAM SYMBOLS COMES FIRST

As you probably know, there are many books on interpreting dreams, but most of them give you a dream dictionary with specific meanings for each symbol. Very few tell you that your symbols are personal. None I know of will show you how to discover what the image means to you, so you can correctly interpret your own dreams. I believe there are very few dream symbols that are truly universal, and those few may have several meanings.

For example, fire is given as a universal symbol in most dream books. But even as a universal symbol it has several very different meanings! It has meant purification, change, destruction, and several other things as well.[1] Suppose someone was once burned very badly in a fire. Then the fire in her dream may mean something different to her, such as fear. Water's universal symbol is often fluidity or Holy Spirit. I love swimming, and water appearing in my dreams often means a relaxed state to me. Someone else may have nearly drowned, and to him water may mean death.

In order to truly interpret your dreams in a way that has specific meaning for you, you must first learn your own dream symbols. You may learn these symbols as you interpret each dream. Even your own symbols may change meaning over time as your consciousness unfolds and expands into new awareness.

An easy way to discover your own symbols is to take it step-by-step each time you have a dream. Try this dream technique. Write your answers here or in your own dream journal.

In order to truly interpret your dreams in a way that has specific meaning for you, you must first learn your own dream symbols.

Dream Technique: T–Technique

1. Draw a line down the center of your paper so you have two sides, right and left, as shown below. On the left side put the key images (symbols) in your dream. It's OK to include feelings, sensations, or anything you are aware of about the dream. Leave the right side blank for now.

    Example: *Jason has a dream where he drinks* water *from a* glass *that's breaking as he drinks. He feels a lot of* fear *about getting hurt. He is standing outside an* elevator.

2. To the right of each word, write the first definition of that word that comes to mind.

    If you have trouble thinking of a definition, pretend you're explaining to a three-year-old or someone from another planet what this thing is. As you repeat the exercise, you may find you'll write the definition just as soon as you have written the symbol. It's perfectly OK to do this exercise in any way that works for you. The whole idea is to be creative!

3. Look at the right side. What does it tell you? If this were my dream, I would say it meant I was feeling fragile and fearful about my sustenance—my life support—in some way. The elevator was the key. I needed to go to a higher level to see the complete picture.

Symbol	Meaning
glass (broken)	fragile
water	sustenance
fear	fear
elevator	takes you to a higher level

USING PRAYER OR CONTEMPLATION TO INTERPRET DREAMS

Whatever the dream, spiritual exercises are a great method of getting to the core of its meaning.

One way to interpret dreams is through spiritual exercises. Eckankar teaches spiritual exercises that anyone, from any religion, can use to strengthen their spiritual senses, open themselves to more divine guidance, and gain a view of life from a much higher perspective.

Whatever the dream, spiritual exercises are a great method of getting to the core of its meaning. Practice this technique for at least thirty days to make sure you've given it enough time to work. This method could take quite a bit of practice, but it is worth every ounce of effort.

Whatever your religion, you were probably taught to either pray, meditate, or contemplate. In this technique you simply read your journal entry for a dream and contemplate on the dream, asking God to help you see the meaning of this dream.

This exercise also includes using a special holy word. Singing this special word always gives me more inner peace and greater understanding. This sacred word is HU. It is sung as a love song to God. This ancient word has been in the ECK teachings and spoken of in other religions throughout history. It's pronounced like the word *hue* and is sung in a long drawn-out breath (HU-u-u-u-u).

HU is in all sounds. Different cultures and religions throughout the world mention HU in one form or another.

To more clearly hear or see the answer to your question, it's important to stay neutral. It helps to say something like, "Thy will be done," to let go of your strong desire to know, so you'll be more receptive to truth.

Be sure to listen very carefully, right there in your contemplative state and throughout the day or week if necessary. God speaks to us constantly, but how often do we listen?

Listening to God means listening to life all around us. What sounds, sights, words, or experiences make you sit up and take notice? Which of these things gives you a clue to solve your own personal riddle?

This exercise includes a special holy word. Singing this word always gives me more inner peace and greater understanding. This sacred word is HU.

Dream Technique: Contemplation Technique

1. Read from your dream journal, and contemplate the dream in question while singing a special love song to God. You can sing HU or your own special prayer to God.

2. Let go by saying, "Thy will be done."

3. Listen very carefully to the Voice of God, the subtle voice within you. Sometimes you can hear this voice in your heart.

4. If you don't feel you have an answer, pick up a holy book or any spiritual book, opening it at random. (Eckankar books are especially good for this; see the back of this book to learn how to request one.) Read the portion that catches your eye, and contemplate on it in relation to your dream. It may give you more insight.

5. Review what you wrote in your dream journal about the dream to see what insights you've gained from going within and listening. Write in your journal any insights you have gotten from any part of this technique.

I had great success with this contemplation technique.

I had great success with this contemplation technique when I had several dreams relating to work. In my outer life, I was confused about what kind of job I could get to supplement my then-small income from book royalties. I was resistant to working at anything that didn't seem directly related to my books.

I wasn't able to clearly interpret the dreams, so I randomly opened the book *The Dream Master,* Mahanta Transcripts, Book 8,[2] by Harold Klemp. This paragraph caught my eye:

> This life provides the experiences needed to become the very best—not in a mechanical, mental way, but spiritually. In the process, you may become very good at your profession or some other facet of life, but what you are really doing is learning to open your heart to love.

I then reread my dream journal and interpreted the dreams based on what I'd read in *The Dream Master.* I needed to open myself to whatever job would build a better spiritual foundation for me, opening my heart to more love. After all, my spiritual goals are the most important goals in my life, and I was losing sight of that. This gentle paragraph reminded me why I'm really here and what's vital in my life.

The Buddy System

Interpreting your own dreams is such a great key to self-discovery. It's what this book is all about. But you may also want to get help with interpreting your dreams or help someone else with theirs if they ask. Here's a way that allows each person to interpret their own dreams without interference.

The buddy system works great if you have a mate, family members, roommates, or close friends who like the idea of working with dreams. Each person acts as a sounding board for the other, when appropriate. I like to share my dreams with people

The buddy system works great if you have a mate, family members, roommates, or close friends who like the idea of working with dreams.

close to me who have open loving hearts and open minds and whose confidentiality I trust.

When my friends or my husband talks about a dream, right away I want to tell them what I think it means. But first I ask, "What do you think it means?" I'm constantly amazed at what happens next. The dreamer almost always comes up with a completely different interpretation than the one I was so sure about!

Now, when someone asks me what I think their dream means, I make myself ask a question about a dream symbol they have mentioned. Say their dream symbol was a microphone. I'll ask, "What does a microphone mean to you?" I might have said it meant a better way to communicate with others, whereas the dreamer may say it represents a fearful experience. You can learn more about your own dreams by interpreting them for yourself. The following technique is one you can use to talk it out and get more insight from your own words.

> You can learn more about your own dreams by interpreting them for yourself.

Dream Technique: Talking It Out

1. Ask your dream buddy to listen while you tell your dream. They must listen and ask questions, such as What do you think the tiger represents? but offer no interpretation.

2. Listen to yourself as you talk. What jumps out at you? As your buddy asks you questions, be aware of insights coming from your answers.

ANOTHER WAY OF INTERPRETING DREAMS—SOMETIMES YOU JUST KNOW

Do you remember a time you just knew something was going to happen or someone was going to call or surprise you? This same feeling of knowing can be applied to dream interpretation. Intuition is something we all have.

Many people, in every kind of situation, are learning to trust their intuition. If you like the idea of experimenting with trusting your inner knowing, try the following dream technique. It is for anyone who would like to develop their intuition.

Intuition is something we all have.

Dream Technique: Direct Knowing

1. Read the journal entry for your dream, all the while saying to yourself, "I know exactly what this dream means." Imagine that when you get to the end of the entry, you will know with certainty what the dream means for you.

2. Write down any insights, no matter how unclear they may seem to you.

3. If you need to do so, reread the entry later that day or the next day to see if you understand the dream on a deeper level or have gained more insight from your experiences during the day. Be patient with yourself and trust completely that you will become an expert at interpreting your dreams.

Jay decided to use this technique for a dream that confused him:

There was a blue jay sitting on an electric wire, and somehow it could not seem to fly away. It was stuck.

Jay reread the entry for this dream, affirming to himself that he would know the meaning of it. He wrote in his journal, "The meaning of this dream is—" and the realization struck him! He wrote quickly without stopping to think or judge what came through to him.

> The blue jay is me, of course, and I'm stuck somewhere, but where? I do know where it is . . . it's at my job! But why blue? I do know why blue . . . because my job is making me feel blue, certainly. Why a wire? I do know the answer to this, the wire is . . . my lifeline, or I thought it was, but really it could kill me if I stayed there long enough. I was meant to fly, I only have to know it!

Jay kept writing to himself that he knew and filling himself with the feeling that he would remember any second what he already knew. He solved his mystery by knowing and imagining he could, and so can you!

Have You Come Up with a Blank?

When I have trouble figuring out what a dream means, even after using some of the above techniques, I ask for more dreams! If you're stumped, try this next technique. I've used it to discover elusive patterns.

When I have trouble figuring out what a dream means, even after using some of the above techniques, I ask for more dreams!

Dream Technique: Asking for More Dreams

1. Imagine you're speaking to God or your inner guide, and say, "Please give me another dream about this situation I've been working with. Please give me a dream I can easily interpret and understand." Write this request in your journal.

   I do this at least one more night, if I need to. I also look at my life to see what messages I may be missing. See chapter 12, "Life Is But a Dream," for more information on how to interpret the dream of life.

DO ALL DREAMS NEED INTERPRETING?

When you find yourself flying in your dreams, experiencing great joy and freedom, you're having a real experience as Soul. Dreams can also give us real experiences that help us expand our spiritual awareness. More about these spiritual experiences is given in later chapters.

Some dream experiences are to prepare us for future experiences. The thought of these future experiences may cause us stress or anxiety. Dreams can help us prepare for these future situations.

Some dreams help heal old wounds or recent traumas. Studies have been done to prove this. An article by Stewart and Koulack of the University of Manitoba, published in *Dreaming,* Journal of the Association for the Study of Dreams, mentioned that

When you find yourself flying in your dreams, experiencing great joy and freedom, you're having a real experience as Soul.

dreams may help people adapt to trauma or stress.[3] To me, such dream experiences are so valuable in the healing process and are necessary for many people to continue to lead a balanced life after experiencing some kind of emotional shock or major physical change. Because of this, I don't feel that these dreams necessarily need interpreting.

Another article, this one by Dr. Ernest Hartmann of Tufts University, also published in *Dreaming, Journal of the Association for the Study of Dreams,* discusses the similarities between dreams and psychotherapy.[4] The article, "Making Connections in a Safe Place: Is Dreaming Psychotherapy?" notes how dreams can help integrate traumatic events, in a way similar to psychotherapy. If such dreams are an outlet and means of healing, I feel they too may not need interpreting.

As you continue with your dream journal and practice some dream techniques, you'll find yourself knowing with more confidence which dreams you need to interpret and which experiences to simply cherish and let be.

Now you have a few tools for unlocking the mysteries of your dreams. How about tackling some of those challenges you're facing right now in your life by using your dreams to solve specific problems? The next chapter shows you how.

How about tackling some of those challenges you're facing right now in your life by using your dreams to solve specific problems?

3

Spiritual Problem Solving through Dreams

At some level Soul knows everything. If there is something that you would like to bring into consciousness, here is a way to get help.

Before you go to sleep, relax and decide that upon awakening you will have an answer to whatever it is that you desire.

When you awaken it will be in the fore-front of your thoughts. At the moment of slipping from or into sleep, you are opened to truth and in direct contact with it. It is at this point that you will perceive your answer.

—Harold Klemp, *The Spiritual Exercises of ECK*[1]

homas Edison used the dream state to solve many problems he ran into with his inventions. When he hit a roadblock, he would sit in his favorite chair holding steel balls in each hand. As soon as he drifted off to sleep his hands relaxed and the balls hit metal pans he'd set under them. He awoke with a jerk, often with an idea for solving the problem.[2]

You can solve problems in your sleep, just like Edison and many other great thinkers. But you don't have to wait for a dream to help you piece together your life's puzzles! You can set the stage before you go to sleep, by setting up the conditions to have a specific dream.

Why feel like a victim of life when you can take responsibility and therefore take charge?

MAKING DECISIONS CAN BE SIMPLER

One way you can take charge is by using the dream state to help you make decisions.

One way you can take charge is by using the dream state to help you make decisions. Our minds love to play tennis with a problem until we tire of the effort. Then we can surrender the problem to Divine Spirit in the dream state. The following story illustrates the point.

Anne had two very good job offers. She was thinking of working in a photography studio. That sounded like fun, but mostly she was interested because of the staff. They seemed very nice, and she even knew one of the people she'd be working with. Still, the other position she was considering was more lucrative, with benefits galore. It seemed like it would be just as enjoyable.

For Anne, the people she worked with were at the top of her priority list. In this case, the deciding factor would be the people. Anne asked for spiritual guidance to help her make the right decision. She used her contemplation/prayer time to ask God to show her which job would be best for her, which would make her happiest and serve Holy Spirit too. Then she had the following dream:

Finding herself in a photography studio's dark-room, Anne looked down at the floor noticing it was made of sand. That might have been acceptable, but it was littered with garbage like an unkempt beach.

The simplicity of this dream struck Anne with the realization that there was some unfinished business she might have to clean up at the photography studio, and that that business was not hers. Anne trusted her dream to show her the reality of the situation beyond appearances.

Anne took the second job, even though she felt a little sad about missing the opportunity to work with her friend. But unexpectedly, the friend left the photography studio within one week. She was replaced by someone Anne had met working at another company. Anne was very much aware that she would have been unhappy working with that person. Anne is now very happy with the position she chose. She made the right decision, based on trust in her spiritual guidance and awareness of the power of her dreams.

If you'd like help with making decisions, using a technique like Anne used, try this next one.

Dream Technique: Sleep On It

1. Think of a question, problem, or decision you need to deal with.

2. Get out your dream journal, and write your question or describe your problem or decision.

Get out your dream journal, and write your question or describe your problem.

Imagine that when you awaken, you will have a smile on your face, saying to yourself, "I know exactly what to do now!" Accompanying your words is a feeling of lightness, happiness that your burden has been lifted.

3. Ask God or the Holy Spirit for help setting up a dream that will give you a clear, direct answer to your question or help with your problem or decision. Sing HU (as explained in chapter 1) or use whatever song or prayer is uplifting to you spiritually. Go to sleep with this prayer or love song to God on your lips.

4. When you awaken, write down every detail of your dream you can remember, even if it seems disjointed or strange. Write down your feelings too. Also note ways you feel more lighthearted, if you do.

YOUR WISEST COUNSEL

You are your own wisest counsel.

You are your own wisest counsel. Please note that when using dreams to make decisions, consult your own common sense as well, including any laws, whether spiritual or physical, that may supersede dream guidance. Listen to your intuition, and look at the circumstances and conditions present at the time of your decision to find your own best answer. A woman we'll call Sally hinged her whole life on one dream, ignoring all else, and was sorry she did.

Sally decided go back to a rocky marriage and try to make it work after this dream:

There was a house that was rotting. The ceiling was full of worms. The roof began caving in. Yet the foundation was still there, and it looked strong.

Sally decided this dream meant her marriage had a strong foundation, even though there were a lot of problems to work out. She went back to her husband but became very ill. The relationship became worse than ever, and no one was happy. Finally, Sally left and her life improved tremendously. She learned to be more independent and loved the progress she made spiritually, learning to be free.

Sally realized in hindsight that her dream really meant she and her husband had a strong spiritual foundation of divine love, but not a good marriage. She had wanted to go back to him so much that she was willing to ignore all the signs steering her away from him. Her interpretation of this dream took her on a detour, but Sally feels good about the lesson she learned: We need to pay attention to all the signs, using dreams as a supplement.

We need to pay attention to all the signs, using dreams as a supplement.

CAREER CHANGES CAN BE MORE COMFORTABLE

It can be challenging to enter a new career or job, as I found out when I went to work selling appliances for a major department store chain. They had every kind of appliance you could imagine, and I had to learn about them all!

There was a two-week training course for each new employee. I was eager to get started but also scared that I wouldn't be able to learn all the details I needed in that time.

I decided to ask for help. As mentioned earlier in the book, in Eckankar we have a personal spiritual guide called the Mahanta. He's also known as the Dream Master because he works with us nightly in our dreams. Anyone can ask the Dream Master to work with them, no matter what their religion.

Anyone can ask the Dream Master to work with them, no matter what their religion.

In the dream state, the Mahanta, or Dream Master, can help us overcome life's many challenges as well as guide us into greater spiritual awareness. Examples of this will be covered in later chapters. For now, we'll talk about how the Dream Master can help us resolve daily problems.

I needed to begin making money as soon as possible in this new position, so I asked the Dream Master to help me learn as quickly as I could by working with this new job in the dream state. Here's what happened:

I dreamed I was on the showroom floor at my new job. I felt very comfortable and at ease with everything. I seemed to know what I needed with every customer. I had the information at my fingertips, or another salesperson was easily available to help me.

The next week flew by, and I devoured every piece of literature I was given to study. The person training me was kind and positive. She encouraged me and gave me confidence in myself. I passed the tests with flying colors. At the end of the week I was told it was time to get started, that I was now finished with training. In just one week I had completed a two-week course!

When I started selling, it felt great. I was still a little hesitant about some things, especially the cash register. There was a very kind young man who was also a salesperson, and he helped me every chance he got. It seemed whenever I was stuck, he was available!

The love of God was with me constantly through the entire time at that job, and I was so grateful.

If you're experiencing jitters or apprehension of any kind, this next dream technique may be of use to you. It's similar to the one I used to help me overcome my fear about my new job.

If you're experiencing jitters or apprehension of any kind, this next dream technique may be of use to you.

Dream Technique: Getting More Comfortable with Challenges Ahead

1. Before going to sleep, write in your dream journal about how you would like to feel in your new job, home, class, or situation. Write everything you can imagine you would think and feel.

2. Next, in your own words, write the following:

    Dear Dream Master (or God, if you prefer), "Please give me a dream or series of dreams to help me move easily and confidently into this new situation."

    Add "Thy will be done" or "Let me know how I can best be of service with love."

    This way, you can let go of the results, allowing the greatest understanding for the good of all to come forth. Use the words that best fit your spiritual philosophy. It's been scientifically proven that when you are neutral

---

or "let go" in your prayers, they work better! In *The Slow Burning Love of God,* Mahanta Transcripts, Book 13,[3] Harold Klemp refers to a study done by the Spindrift Organization where plant growth was increased by praying, but even more so with the prayer, "Thy will be done."

3. Upon awakening, write down your dream. Even if you only remember a word, image, or feeling, write about that.

4. Later, be sure to write about how the situation turned out and whether the dream helped you feel more confident or comfortable.

Upon awakening, write down your dream. Even if you only remember a word, image, or feeling, write about that.

FOR SOLVING PROBLEMS, DREAMS CAN'T BE BEAT

My mind sure likes to get in the way when I have a challenge to face. When faced with major decisions, I've been known to let my mind run wild for great lengths of time. I get more confused than ever when I do this, allowing an imperfect tool (the mind) to give me direction that can only come clearly from the higher self, Soul. Dreams have been my best resource for overcoming this and bringing about a solution to problems or decisions.

Between the time I got the advance for my first book, *Think Yourself Thin,*[4] and my first royalty check, two years had passed. The advance was used up the first year to pay debts and living expenses while I promoted my book. I was running out of money. I was wondering how I'd make it financially without a job, a job that could take me away from my dream.

I thought about going back into freelance consulting for small businesses. It made sense to me. I'd only need a few clients on retainer for a few months. No problem, easy solution. Somehow, though, it felt heavy. I felt a deep sadness that I'd be focusing in the wrong direction, away from my goal of helping many people through writing. I decided to ask the Dream Master for help. Here are the dreams I got during the next few days:

1. *My editor was working on more projects, helping to organize something.*
2. *I was going on location with two crews from a television station to film something. There was a reporter there that I was attracted to.*
3. *I met some guys who were going to help a friend buy a new Mercedes Benz so his family could feel rich and be successful thereafter.*

The first dream was telling me I could work on another book project. The second dream was indicating that PR was a good focus for my attention. The third dream meant all of the above would put me in a position to be prosperous, and that I should keep thinking positive, prosperous thoughts.

The dreams were indeed guiding me in a good direction, since I did get added PR from my publicist and I also got support from friends who believed in me and what I was doing. Attendance at my workshops increased and orders kept coming in for books and tapes that I publish myself.

> I decided to ask the Dream Master for help.

Although I still had a few challenges in this area, Holy Spirit—what we in Eckankar call "the ECK," the essence of God—has continually guided me toward the means to support myself as I serve God in the way I feel directed.

YOU MAY NOT GET IMAGES OF DREAMS, BUT FEELINGS WORK JUST AS WELL

When I decided I would continue to focus on being an author and workshop leader until my next royalty check or advance, I took a deep breath. Then I thought of the worst thing that could happen: I'd be homeless!

Knowing it would probably never happen, I immediately called my best friend and asked, "If I focus on my goal of being a successful author and I can't pay rent for a while, can I live in your guest room and pay my way by cooking and cleaning?"

Without even pausing, she said, "Of course!"

I was laughing by then and so was she. She knew it was very unlikely that her hospitality would be needed but was still willing to go along with my backup plan.

My mind was now settled and relaxed, so I went to work on my dreams. That night I asked for a dream to show me what to do about my finances.

I did not remember the dream, but I woke up with the feeling that I was very secure. The inner peace was so pervasive, I couldn't figure out why I had ever worried. Still, I couldn't remember the dream. I had to trust my inner knowing.

That night I asked for a dream to show me what to do about my finances.

Soul knows all, sees all, and has no fear. The awareness of Soul often comes through, even without the dream images.

That morning I found three more people to help me get through the financial obstacle course and was very grateful for their support and belief in me. I hung in there, and my financial base stabilized so I could continue to be of service in the way I love.

For any decision making or problem solving in the dream state, use the Sleep On It technique given earlier in this chapter.

Another dreamer made a decision based on the feeling alone.

In a fairly new marriage, Georgia was concerned about contributing her share to the family income. She had a young teenage son and felt responsible for his welfare. She didn't want to burden her new husband too much. Georgia was searching for the perfect job or business opportunity, one that would afford her the freedom of being available to her son on a daily basis, allow time for her new husband, and bring in a good income.

Georgia did find a job, but it was draining her time and energy and left little time for her family or herself. She kept an eye open for better opportunities. When her former boyfriend approached her with what seemed like a golden business opportunity, she was very tempted. Talking it over with her husband, she sensed that he wasn't too keen on the idea of her working with her former beau. She was somewhat distraught about her husband's discomfort, though it seemed mild.

For any decision making or problem solving in the dream state, use the Sleep On It technique given earlier in this chapter.

That night Georgia asked for a dream to help her decide what to do, since she felt so torn. She asked her inner Dream Master, "Should I start this business with my friend?"

When she awoke, she had no recollection of any dreams. However, an image began to form in her mind, a thought: *something sticky, like a spider's web.*

It came from the profound feeling of knowing that this business opportunity, though an OK business, would be completely wrong for her. Her dream message was a definite "No." There was no doubt, because whenever she put her attention on the business, she felt a wave of nausea.

Georgia looked over at her husband who was still sleeping, and her heart swelled with love for him. At that moment she simply knew that she could not do anything to disrupt the precious harmony of her family, which was the present and the future. Her family was an expression of divine love, a precious gift.

Georgia knew involvement with this ex-boyfriend would be like a sticky spider's web. She trusted the feelings she had when she woke up. Even though she couldn't remember the dream, she let her feelings guide her.

Dreams can shine light on those shadowy specters in our lives.

Discovering Roadblocks through Dreams

There are times we have roadblocks that are invisible to us. Mine are often visible to everyone but me! Dreams can shine light on those shadowy specters in our lives.

Long ago I had a relationship with someone I trusted completely. Because of my youth and naïveté, I went along blithely until I began having dreams of his being a thief.

In one dream:

He was in an upstairs apartment, my apartment, tossing valuable equipment and furniture to a friend below who placed it on a truck to be sold later.

When I awoke from this dream, I knew something was wrong but didn't want to face it for fear of losing the love I had finally found, not knowing it was not love at all, but need. He would have preyed on that need by taking from me in ways I wouldn't have noticed. The very tangible experience I got that validated the dream was he never paid back money he'd borrowed from me, even though we'd parted on friendly terms.

Thank goodness I listened to my dream and finally accepted the truth it was trying to convey to me. Had I listened more carefully to earlier messages from Divine Spirit, I would have been free of the situation sooner. Here's a technique that could help you see early warning signs.

Had I listened more carefully to earlier messages from Divine Spirit, I would have been free of the situation sooner.

Dream Technique: Watching for Road Signs and Roadblocks

1. Look through your dream journal to find any dreams that may not fit your present perception of a situation or person, as in my dream.

2. Ask yourself if the dream fits your truest inner feeling or intuition about the person or situation. Write these feelings and thoughts in your dream journal. This may be difficult to face if you've been denying your feelings, like I did. Give yourself time to let the truth filter in.

3. Pray, meditate, or contemplate on what your next step should be. Ask for guidance from your spiritual teacher, guardian angel, or God. If you need help getting a clear, high perspective, try singing HU, as described in chapter 1.

4. If you still don't feel you have a clear answer, ask for more dreams about this topic so you may have more material to work with.

Dreams can pull us out of the mental arena of fear into the world of Soul, into the light of truth.

DREAMS MAY HELP US OVERCOME FEARS AND MAKE BETTER DECISIONS

When faced with confusing or difficult decisions, dreams can be the voice of truth. The human mind tends to run in circles. Like a hamster on a wheel, the mind often takes us nowhere. Dreams can pull us out of the mental arena of fear into the world of Soul, into the light of truth. One example of how this can work was an experience Gillian had.

Gillian was thinking about a decision she needed to make regarding her working partnership with Delores. As of late, Gillian had been taking on more responsibility in the company, yet her monetary compensation hadn't increased. She was not happy, but didn't feel able to talk to Delores about it quite yet.

Gillian was very good at keeping her dream journal and spent time in the morning writing her dreams. She was quite intrigued by the following one:

Gillian had been invited to Delores's home for brunch. Delores's parents were visiting when Gillian arrived at the designated time, so Delores asked her business partner to wait. Gillian wandered into the kitchen to get a glass of water. There stood a young woman she didn't recognize and a man who was berating the girl quite savagely. He was cruel. Gillian said to him, "There's plenty of love around for everyone, and everyone deserves that love and respect!"

After that comment, he became very vicious, coming at the young woman with sharp objects. Gillian ignored this. She was feeling hungry, so she went into the other room, where brunch should have been ready, but found that her host had already eaten. Gillian realized that Delores didn't really care whether Gillian had eaten or not, even though Gillian was her guest and she had invited her!

Gillian didn't have much trouble interpreting this dream. She knew that it was telling her that Delores didn't really care about Gillian's needs. However, there was another piece to this dream she recognized as being part of herself. The young woman was the part of her that stood by, while the man was the part that was not treating herself very well at all. She knew now she needed to take action, rather than walking out on herself, like she had in the dream. She decided to ask for what she wanted.

The action Gillian took gave her back her self-respect and brought her new respect from Delores in

She knew now she needed to take action, rather than walking out on herself, like she had in the dream.

the way of increased income and better working hours. Gillian found she could have asked for what she needed earlier and probably would have gotten it, had she been able to overcome her fear and take better care of herself. Gillian was learning the spiritual qualities of taking responsibility for what happened to her, loving herself more, and being free.

If you would like to overcome the fears in your life right now, try this next exercise tonight:

Dream Technique: Facing Dragons

1. Identify the fear. Is it talking with your boss about that time off you need or discussing a new car purchase with your mate? Could it be quitting a job you feel finished with or moving to a new city? Ask yourself, "What's so scary about this?" Ultimately, the fear of death is the fear that underlies almost every other fear we have. We'll call your primary fear in this situation the "dragon."

2. When you have been able to find the "dragon," ask for guidance in your dreams to help you face this fear and vanquish it, or at least befriend it. Give love to the dragon in any way you can and go to sleep knowing that you will reach an agreement with it or find a way to see past it to the solution.

3. As usual, write in your dream journal any words (no matter how few), images, or feelings

---

Ultimately, the fear of death is the fear that underlies almost every other fear we have.

you recognize upon arising. Do this for as many nights as needed until you feel balanced inside about this situation.

Whenever life hands you a challenge, you can rise to the occasion by consulting the wisdom of your dreams.

Many of the difficulties in life are resolved through dreams producing subtle or astounding healing. In the next chapter you will see how others received healing more directly through dreams, and how you may do so as well.

Whenever life hands you a challenge, you can rise to the occasion by consulting the wisdom of your dreams.

4

The Miraculous Healing Power of Dreams

If you understand dreams and how they work, you can use your dreams to take the next step in your own life.

— Harold Klemp, *How the Inner Master Works,*
Mahanta Transcripts, Book 12[1]

HEALING IN DREAMS IS AN ANCIENT TECHNIQUE

In ancient Greece, people gathered every night, waiting to sleep in temples and holy places. Why? Because they wanted a dream healing, and the temples were believed to be the best place for that. After all, it was holy ground!

Yet, I believe holy ground is really wherever you are. The Dream Master will visit you whenever you ask. And a dream healing may be yours if you request it with a loving, open heart and it does not interfere with your spiritual unfoldment as Soul.

The Dream Master will visit you whenever you ask.

Joe had a foot fungus which refused to go away, even after he had diligently used all of the suggested products on the market. He tried more natural remedies which helped for a time, but then the fungus would return. It wasn't a comfortable state of affairs. Joe was used to working with his dreams, so he finally tried them as a last resort. One night he asked the Dream Master for a healing. This is what happened in a dream:

As he was lying on a bed, Joe looked down at his feet and saw a golden light surrounding them. They began to feel warm and comfortable, unlike anything he had ever felt. The light was so soothing it rocked him to sleep.

When Joe awoke, he knew his feet had been healed. He could scarcely believe it when he looked at them, for there was absolutely no trace of the fungus that had been there the night before!

SOME DREAMS GIVE US THE MEANS TO HEAL OURSELVES

Not everyone has a dream healing as dramatic as Joe's, but they're no less effective. The resolution of some health issues through dreams comes in dream symbols that suggest a new way of eating or exercise or lifestyle changes.

Without even asking for help with his health, Gary had a dream that was showing him danger ahead if he didn't change a certain eating pattern. In his dream:

He was standing on a dock, watching men load large crates into the hold of a ship. One load was particularly heavy, and the machinery could not lift it. Gary looked closer and saw that the crate was loaded with chocolate.

The resolution of some health issues through dreams comes in dream symbols that suggest a new way of eating or exercise or lifestyle changes.

When Gary awoke, it was very clear to him that he needed to quit eating so much chocolate! His body was the machinery, and the chocolate was "holding him down" from optimum health.

Karen had a humorous dream about her chocolate cravings:

While spying on a chocolate factory, she saw the factory workers eating carrots while they were working, not chocolate. Karen found out that they were making chocolate to control the rest of the world!

That helped her to realize she was being controlled by the chocolate. She admitted she would eat the whole box if it was in her home, so she decided to buy just one piece at a time.

Another example of warnings about potential health hazards was a dream a health practitioner had. He loves coffee. Even though he knew the caffeine was not good for him, he allowed himself a cup only every so often. The only problem was the "every so oftens" were coming too often! He had several dreams, along with the feeling he should quit. Here's one of the dreams:

The health practitioner ordered an espresso in a nice restaurant where the coffee should have been of excellent quality. He began to take his first sip and spit it out in disgust. It tasted exactly like turpentine.

After this dream, the man knew it was time to slow down on the coffee.

After this dream, the man knew it was time to slow down on the coffee, but he didn't quit completely. There was one more time he enjoyed himself and indulged in a cup of coffee with some friends.

The coffee arrived, and he caught the aroma. It was slightly off. As he drank it, he realized it tasted a little funny. He told me later that, "Because it was coffee, I insisted on drinking it." He was very sorry he had. He had a stomachache all night long. He swore that was his last cup of coffee for a long, long time!

Now this healer is healing himself by cutting out the coffee except on rare occasions. He has seen a definite improvement in his health that he attributes to this discipline.

YOU MAY BE DIRECTED
TOWARD A DIFFERENT DOCTOR

When Tracy was in college she had a lot of shoulder and back pain. She went to a physical therapist at the campus health center but got little results. The pain persisted.

What could she do?

Tracy knew about a new deep-massage technique that seemed to help people with long-standing pain. Should she try this new treatment? She wasn't sure. Then Tracy dreamed:

> *She was visiting a man who had a wonderful toolkit which he used to help people lead more comfortable lives.*

As soon as she woke up, Tracy knew she was to try the new massage method. The person she'd been referred to was a man, and the tools in the dream were his hands. She did go to see him, and the massage worked for her!

As soon as she woke up, Tracy knew she was to try the new massage method.

So many different ways of eating, exercising, and healing are available in the world. Who's to know what's best for your particular body and at this time in your life? Of course, Holy Spirit knows. And as Soul, a manifestation of Holy Spirit yourself, you know. Getting this through to the mind can be quite challenging, however. Try using the dream state to fill in the missing puzzle pieces. Use common sense and known resources. Ask for help in any way you know how.

> Try using the dream state to fill in the missing puzzle pieces. Ask for help in any way you know how.

SOME DREAM HEALING BEGINS WITH IMAGINING OURSELVES WELL

When I was writing *Think Yourself Thin,* I interviewed several women who had used a dream technique I had suggested. The technique helps people accept a new body by setting up a scenario in the dream state where they can more easily imagine it. They can actually experience their new healthy, slim selves. Here are two examples of how it works.

Laura asked to experience what it would feel like to have her ideal body: light, happy, and free. She had a dream of a little girl swinging on a doorknob.

Laura realized she had done that often as a little girl of three. The memory helped her get into the very feeling she was trying to create. It worked!

Remembering her childlike feelings helped Laura get in touch with the spiritual gift of imagination, creating a new life as well as a new body.

Susan was surprised by her dream of a sleek, white sports car.

It felt good to feel so aerodynamic. She could move with ease and grace, feeling slim and beautiful all the while. After thinking about it, the dream fit perfectly. She is moving toward that sleek self with ease, knowing that the inner feeling of being aerodynamic and light was the most important piece of the picture. That lighter feeling may have represented her as a spiritual being, Soul, as well as her new body.

You can use your divine gift of imagination to create more health for yourself too.

Dream Technique: Asking for Healing

1. Write down your health ideal. Use only positive words that evoke an image you *want,* such as *healthy, comfortable* (instead of pain-free), *clear and clean* (instead of smoke-free), *slim, strong, energetic,* etc. Read *Think Yourself Thin* or other books on positive imaging, like *The Flute of God*[2] by Paul Twitchell, so you can understand the importance of positive images in communication with the subconscious.

2. Ask for dreams to help you get comfortable with the new you, accepting your new state of health. For most of us, it's difficult to let go of the limiting patterns in our lives. After all, the mind loves to run in a groove, just like the needle on a phonograph record! Remember to let go of any control, and let Holy Spirit do the work, since It knows much better than we do what we need.

Remember to let go of any control, and let Holy Spirit do the work, since It knows much better than we do what we need.

3. Enjoy those dreams and especially any feeling of joy or lightness that goes with them. The *feeling* is the secret to creating a new life.

4. Revisit the dream to feel those great feelings and believe they're yours! Health issues can be resolved in the dream state with surprising healing.

Health issues can be resolved in the dream state with surprising healing.

RELATIONSHIPS CAN BE BEGUN OR IMPROVED THROUGH DREAMS

Katy wanted to find the right relationship in the worst way. She decided to begin a special journal just for that purpose. She made a contract with herself and with God to do whatever it might take to find this love in her life. She was told by the Mahanta, her inner spiritual guide, that she must be willing to move away from the city she lived in and loved. Katy made a commitment to make note of every dream, waking dream (see chapter 12), and realization regarding this topic. She asked for dreams about her mate, the one she knew was coming into her life. Here's what Katy experienced:

She began to dream about a man dressed all in black leather with a ponytail and one earring, who was riding a motorcycle. This was not her kind of man. A business suit, neatly trimmed hair, and a BMW were more her style. She kept saying to herself, "I'm in love with him?"

For two years Katy watched her life change as she worked with her journal and her dreams. She decided to do everything in her power to become more relaxed with life, more in love with life itself. As she did this, she had more and more dreams about the man on the motorcycle. One day, a male friend of two years was traveling through Katy's city and stayed with her as usual, sleeping on her couch. That night she had another dream about her man in leather whose face she'd never seen before in these dreams.

This time she saw his face and recognized it as her friend. The Mahanta, the Dream Master, said to her, "Your true companion is in the other room."

She was in shock as she realized it was the very same friend who was fast asleep on her couch. She ran into the living room and looked down at him, shaking her head thinking, "I'm in love with you?"

Throughout that day, she observed him carefully, watching everything he did and realized that everything he did was like magic to her! She just knew he was the one for her. Katy began to realize they had an incredible relationship. He began to see it too. Their friendship had always been a very special one. For two years they had built the strongest foundation any romance could have: a solid friendship.

Would you like to create better relationships in your life?

Within one week they were happily in love, and in three months they were married. And yes, Katy did have to move away from her beloved home in Minnesota to Canada, his home, but got to return to her hometown with him two years later.

Would you like to create better relationships in your life? Try the technique below, remembering that patience is the golden key.

Dream Technique: Creating a New Relationship in Your Life

1. Decide what kind of new relationship you want to create in your life, and write it down in your own words. Perhaps it's a good friend, a companion to have fun with, a mate, or even a loving pet. It could even be improving the relationships you already have.

   If you wish to try Katy's method, make a contract with yourself and God in your dream journal that you are committed to doing whatever it will take to make this happen.

2. Ask for dreams to help you step into that new state of being, accepting the love and blessings it will bring.

   You can experience new states of consciousness and begin to put on the new cloak of higher levels of love in the dream state. Imagine yourself taking on new positive attitudes.

   You may find your life taking a turn and old thoughts, attitudes, or opinions being worked out of you or just dropping away.

3. Watch your dreams and begin to get the feel for this new state of being. Try to live in a state of being in love, or "being in happiness" as much as you can. Watch the miracles occur—from healing old wounds to being delighted with your life just as it is!

Imagine yourself taking on new positive attitudes.

HEALING RELATIONSHIP ISSUES
THROUGH DREAMS

I had a pattern of getting involved with unbalanced relationships, whether platonic or romantic. What I mean by this is that I felt I was doing all the giving. It seemed to me that little was being returned by the other person in the relationship.

I kept asking for help with this, but until I was ready to face my deepest fear I simply couldn't see the answer. That fear was that I could end up being alone the rest of my life. Finally, I got to the point where it was more painful to keep getting my heart broken than to face the fear of loneliness. I was now willing to look at my pattern and change it in any way I could. I had the following dream:

> I was driving down the road. Some men were in the car with me. They seemed to be friends of a sort, and I was attracted to one of them. The road was very rough, so it was a bumpy ride. We stopped at a construction site. The men got out, stumbling around in the mud and generally acting immature. I began to see them in a different light. I realized I could be having a much nicer time all by myself than with a bunch of half-grown men. I quickly jumped into the driver's seat and took off for the beach to enjoy myself, by myself.

When I awoke from the dream, I felt so free! I knew it meant I could be enjoying life more by myself (even though I felt afraid) than I would by hanging on to immature relationships. I spent the next year by myself most of the time, refusing to go on a date with anyone until I learned to love my own company!

I kept asking for help with this, but until I was ready to face my deepest fear I simply couldn't see the answer.

It worked! I became happier and happier by myself, knowing I had the love of God surrounding me constantly. The Mahanta's presence in my waking life and in my dreams guided me toward a greater awareness every day of the love surrounding me. I had to realize the most basic relationship I needed to cultivate was my relationship with God. As soon as I accepted the Mahanta's love in all my waking moments, I realized he gives me more love than I'd ever gotten from or given anyone. Here was my perfect relationship!

Once I relaxed into the rhythm of love in my life, miracles began to occur. Friendships blossomed, and family members began to visit and call. I felt like I was part of the world again, in a different, more hopeful way than ever before. Finally, I found a best friend who gives in our relationship as much or more than I do.

> I had to realize the most basic relationship I needed to cultivate was my relationship with God.

BEING HONEST WITH YOURSELF IS VITAL TO SUCCESS

It's impossible to resolve patterns that we're not ready to face. Being honest may take time. Be patient with yourself as you unfold in your awareness of the truth. Be gentle with yourself as you realize the changes that you need to make. When you shine your light on them, the changes will come about naturally, in the time that's best for you and all of life around you.

RECOGNIZING WHERE THE PROBLEM COMES FROM

Patterns like the one I just mentioned can be very frustrating, until we realize we're the ones controlling our own individual universes, for better or worse. It may seem that the other person in a relationship is being unkind or uncaring, and maybe they are. However, when people like that are in our lives, it's generally to wake us up to our own patterns.

The most exciting part is you can have control of your life from the higher viewpoint of Soul. You can see where your attitudes or emotions can be changed to create a whole new scenario.

How can you tell if it is your issue to resolve or the other person's? How can you recognize the source of the problem?

One trick I've found to know where the problem comes from is to ask myself, Who has the emotional reaction in this situation? It's hard to admit it's me! It's often both people, because life is so economical. Both people usually get to learn their spiritual lessons at the same time!

For example: I used to get very agitated in restaurants when the meal I ordered didn't appear in front of me within a certain amount of time. I would complain to my companions with comments like, "What poor service!"

Likewise, I felt the same anxiety at a dinner party when the meal wasn't served as scheduled. I'd think, *I'm starving, I wonder when we'll eat?* or *I didn't come here to watch her cook!*

It took years for me to recognize my own reaction to all of these varied situations. No one else was reacting under the same circumstances. I was reacting to an old pattern! I feel I was neglected as a baby and not fed when needed, so I still had a subconscious fear of starving.

You can see where your attitudes or emotions can be changed to create a whole new scenario.

I often find, when I'm honest with myself, that it's me who is reacting, even when I'm so sure the other person was wrong or at fault. It can be quite embarrassing to discover this; but I try to learn and grow from it, ultimately moving ahead toward giving myself and others more love.

Would you like to resolve some pattern in your own life? Try the following dream technique.

Dream Technique: Letter to God

1. Get out your dream journal, and write down your feelings about a pattern in your life, just as if you are telling your dearest friend. You could even write a letter to God. Here's an example:

   Dear God,

   I am so hurt that this happened again. My heart gets broken every time I trust someone. I give all I can and get nothing back.

2. Ask for help in healing this through your dream state. Do this for as many nights as it takes to help you get through it.

3. Surrender, and trust completely that this will be done, no matter how long it takes.

4. Look for changes in this pattern, no matter how small they may be. Give yourself time to work through it. However, don't limit yourself, as some people have a miraculous healing from just one dream!

Get out your dream journal, and write down your feelings about a pattern in your life, just as if you are telling your dearest friend.

WHAT IF YOU LOSE SOMEONE NEAR TO YOU?

No one can live on earth without losing a loved one at one time or another. Whether through death or distance, separation or growing up, losing love can be a painful and very emotional experience. To ease this emotional stress and tension, and to help heal the pain, you can use dreams.

Proponents of modern self-help and psychology movements are discovering the importance of dreams during traumatic or stressful times. An article, published in *Dreaming,* suggests dreams "may facilitate adaptation to stressful waking events by activating habitual defensive patterns or providing opportunities to integrate stressful new material with earlier solutions to similar problems."[3] Another article in the same publication compared stressful dreams and the dreamer's stress in waking life using data dating as far back as the year 1709.[4] The article by Hartmann mentioned in chapter 2 comparing dreaming to psychotherapy comments that REM sleep with its muscular immobilization provides a safe place for the dreamer to act out in order to integrate a trauma into the dreamer's life.[5]

The good news is, you don't have to make it happen. Just open yourself to the healing power of your dreams. This very thing happened to Dottie.

Dottie knew that her daughter would leave home soon. She was getting ready for college and looking for an apartment fifty miles from home. To Dottie, it seemed like a million miles away. Her daughter was growing up and leaving home. Dottie felt only heartache and loneliness. Her daughter had been

Just open yourself to the healing power of your dreams.

Dottie's only family. How would she cope? Dottie did think of one solution. Dreams! She'd always faithfully recorded her dreams and made a little bit of sense out of some of them. She noticed she felt very different after she woke up from certain dreams.

Dottie decided to ask for a healing dream. She talked with God often, so this night she said, "God, please give me a dream to help me let go of my daughter and heal my heart." Then she went to sleep. This was what she dreamed:

Her daughter was married, living in a house filled with a lot of light and love. Dottie was visiting, and in her arms she was holding a beautiful baby girl, who looked so much like her daughter. It was her granddaughter! Dottie was filled with so much love at that moment that it overflowed from her heart in a shower of little golden hearts, making her granddaughter giggle and smile.

Dottie awoke from this dream with a whole new perspective. She was still filled with lightness and love, and there was something more. She was motivated! She was inspired to help her daughter get out into the world, find her niche, and find her love— so that she could hold that granddaughter! Dottie wouldn't push, though. There was too much love from this dream to let her do anything that would jeopardize her relationship with her daughter. She was just happy.

Even though she'd still miss her daughter's companionship very much, Dottie now knew there was always more love to look forward to. She'd discovered

Dottie decided to ask for a healing dream: "God, please give me a dream to help me let go of my daughter and heal my heart."

the tapestry of God's love that weaves its pattern continually.

Others have found this same sense of love and wonder when they meet a deceased loved one in the dream state for a game of golf or to go dancing. If you want to visit a departed loved one in your dreams, see chapter 9.

THE ULTIMATE PROBLEM-SOLVING TECHNIQUE — MEET YOUR GUARDIAN ANGEL OR THE DREAM MASTER IN YOUR DREAMS

Spiritual beings work with you in your dreams. In Eckankar, the Mahanta, the Dream Master, is our spiritual guide.

Whatever religion you choose to follow, it will have some reference in its holy books to angels or angelic beings. They are said to guide and protect us as agents for God, and they often do so in dreams. Encountering one of these beings is truly a spiritual blessing for those who accept their love and guidance.

Sarah decided she wanted to meet her guardian angel in a dream. She asked for a dream to help her see the presence she always felt so near, so protective. In her dream:

Sarah saw a being bathed in golden light, neither man nor woman, but somehow both. The image left her speechless with love and gratitude.

Sarah now knows that she's surrounded and protected by love and feels this presence of love every day.

I am eternally grateful for the countless times the Mahanta has helped me as my inner spiritual

Spiritual beings work with you in your dreams.

guide. When I need help in the dream state, I ask him for it. I ask to see him in my dreams when I need to be reassured of his love and support.

It's amazing how wonderful it feels to know that I constantly have that loving presence in my life. You can have it too, in whatever way is comfortable for you. Ask your guardian angel or the Mahanta, the Dream Master, to introduce himself to you in your dreams. In the next chapter and in chapter 11, there is more about spiritual experiences in dreams, but for now you can try this exercise.

Ask your guardian angel or the Mahanta, the Dream Master, to introduce himself to you in your dreams.

Dream Technique: Finding Your Guardian Angel

1. Write down why you would like a spiritual guide or guardian angel, if you don't already have one. You may have a guardian angel or guide and not know it!

2. Ask to see him or her in your dreams.

3. Be aware of how you feel when you awake or what images you see.

THE SECRET FREEDOM OF CREATING YOUR DREAMS

In your dreams, you are all-powerful, all-knowing, and all-loving. Why? Because in your dreams, you're free of your body. You are Soul, unlimited by time, space, or matter, unlike your physical body. Your divine gift is imagination. You can create your dreams using this gift that children so readily accept.

I love to dance, so in my dreams I dance in the air. It's so freeing! I can dance while I'm flying, not limited by a stage or a floor. Suppose you want to ride a winged horse or swim with dolphins? Perhaps climbing Mt. Everest appeals to you, or maybe you prefer the speed of the fastest race car you could imagine. Why not have all of the adventures you want in your dreams? The only limits we have in the dream state are those we place on ourselves.

This means you can use your dreams to uplift yourself, heal yourself, and move into new ways of acting or being. If you've been practicing some of the dream techniques given so far, you may be well aware of this already.

A key to making dreams work for you is in letting go and relaxing. You can think of what you'd like to experience, resolve, prepare for, or heal in your dreams and then surrender your desire to God. Then the very best experience for your spiritual unfoldment will occur.

As Soul, you live in the heavenly worlds and on earth at the same time. Your dreams will help you connect your inner and outer life. The next chapter will help you see how this is possible.

As Soul, you live in the heavenly worlds and on earth at the same time. Your dreams will help you connect your inner and outer life.

5

As Above, So Below

By the universal nature of dreams, *I mean that dreams are working continuously in our lives. They are working not only when we are asleep but also when we are awake. The universal nature of dreams encompasses the universal being, Soul.*

— Harold Klemp, *The Dream Master,* Mahanta Transcripts, Book 8[1]

HOW IS IT THAT DREAMS SEEM SO REAL AT TIMES?

Dreams often seem to be real experiences because they are real experiences. Dreams take place in your inner worlds, which are real—they're your inner reality, your own personal state of consciousness. In essence, dreams are your very own window to heaven.

The many levels of heaven lie within us. Thus we hold a key to heaven in our dreams.

An example of a dream that happened in an inner world or heaven and then here on earth was when

Dreams often seem to be real experiences because they are real experiences.

Julia first met and started dating her husband-to-be, Philip. While you read her dream, keep in mind that Julia is an architect:

Julia walked into a crystal palace. It was gorgeous on the outside, and as she entered, the beauty extended inside as well. Someone escorted her around to show her that the castle was incomplete and needed some work. First she was shown that the foyer needed a few small touches here and there. Next, she was taken to a room that needed framing (support structure). Last, they entered a room that had a raw dirt floor.

Julia felt that the crystal palace represented her relationship with Philip. She knew from this dream that there would be some work to do on the relationship before it was complete and ready for marriage. It wouldn't take long, except for the part of their relationship symbolized by the room with the dirt floor. That was the room they would work on together.

This dream experience was very real to Julia. She knew that she was being shown by the Dream Master, in a way she could comprehend, what kind of relationship she would have with Philip. This would help her move forward with confidence, able to pass the spiritual test of patience during the relationship renovation process.

Julia and her husband have now been married for over ten years, and their relationship continues to blossom with a bright and shining love between them.

She knew that she was being shown by the Dream Master, in a way she could comprehend, what kind of relationship she would have with Philip.

Some Cultures View Dreams as Real Experiences

It's interesting to note that some cultures view dreams as real experiences and have a great respect for them. A cross-cultural study of dreams was done at Saybrook Institute and published by the Association for the Study of Dreams.[2] The comparisons of modern dream experts to Native Americans was quite eye opening. In this comparison ten questions were asked about dreams. To illustrate, here are answers to a question from the study, What is the source of dreams?

Answers from modern dream experts:

"Freud: Dreams come from the unconscious, which contains repressed desires.

Jung: Dreams come from the unconscious, which contains the undeveloped aspects of the psyche.

Ullman: Dreams come from the unconscious, which consists of material that dreamers ignore or repress."

Answers from Native Americans:

Hurons: "Our souls have other desires which are, as it were, inborn and concealed . . . They believe that our soul makes these natural desires known by means of dreams, which are its language."

Alaskan Eskimos: "Dreams are a sign that one's soul is wandering."

It's interesting to note that some cultures view dreams as real experiences and have a great respect for them.

Blackfoot: "It is believed that dreams are produced by dream spirits who manifest themselves in dreams as messengers, often in animal form."

Crow: "Dreams come from the spirit world."

Dakota Sioux: "Dreams are believed to be revelations from the spirit world."

Many native cultures believe that dreams are real, spiritual experiences. You can prove this to yourself by delving into dream study as if you believe that your nightly adventures are real. By practicing dream techniques, and by continually asking for divine guidance with your dreams while paying close attention to them.

WHO IS REALLY DREAMING?

If you are sleeping, then who is experiencing the dream? Of course your mind and emotions are involved in the dream, while your eyes move rapidly, as if following the action. But who is observing all of this and experiencing it? The real you, of course, Soul.

Here's proof. Close your eyes, and imagine a dog. Make the dog do all kinds of tricks. Now get yourself involved. Imagine you are doing this, not just observing it. Grab a leash, and take the dog for a walk. Feel the pull of the leash as the dog strains forward, trying to run. Feel the wind in your face, and smell the spring flowers in bloom all around you. See their bright colors and sense the feeling you have right now. Isn't it nice to be out in the fresh air and sunshine?

If your body was sitting still, who is experiencing all of that?

You are—as Soul.

If you are sleeping, then who is experiencing the dream?

You are a very special, unique being. The mind can only feed back to us what we've experienced, but Soul can create beauty that is not found in this everyday world. We can live with that feeling more often if we get in touch with who we really are. There are books that can help you understand more about this if you're interested. One I recommend is called *35 Golden Keys to Who You Are & Why You're Here,* by Linda Anderson.[3]

The mind can only feed back to us what we've experienced, but Soul can create beauty that is not found in this everyday world.

DREAMS ARE REAL EXPERIENCES

I believe dreams are real and they are one way God speaks to us. Sometimes dreams include images of experiences we are having in the heavenly worlds while we sleep.

Here's one more tidbit to help you take this all in. Contrary to popular belief that a long dream experience takes only a few minutes, dream time appears to be the same as real time. When you are dreaming, it's just as though you're having the experience here in the physical world, with the same time frame. This was researched by William C. Dement, a psychiatrist at New York's Mt. Sinai Hospital, around 1959.[4] Dement was a former student of Nathaniel Kleitman (who set up one of the first sleep labs).

According to Harold Klemp in his book *What Is Spiritual Freedom?* Mahanta Transcripts, Book 11:[5] "We know in ECK that the dream worlds are very real; they're not imagination. They are places as solid as the physical. The only difference is that most people are aware of only the physical world."

Many people are aware of their dreams as real experiences because of their dramatic effect on their waking lives.

Many people are aware of their dreams as real experiences because of their dramatic effect on their waking lives.

Someone we'll call Angela had a dream that she later realized was a real experience. This occurred during a particularly difficult time with her stepdaughter, Terra, and the child's mother. Angela decided to seek spiritual counseling. She had a dream following a spiritual counseling session with a clergy member of Eckankar. This was her dream:

Angela took Terra to a park, and they were playing and having fun when a very kind man walked up to them and handed Angela something quite pretty. The man called it a "medicine ball." Angela thanked him profusely for this beautiful gift, then decided she should give it to Terra. Terra was so happy, she was jumping around and playfully running into the street. Just then, along came Terra's mother to pick her up. Terra's mom thanked Angela with a warm smile and went on her way.

This dream was so real to Angela, she felt as if a healing had taken place when she awoke. Angela realized this dream meant that any rift between her and Terra's mother had been healed. The beautiful medicine ball was the gift of healing in a way her mind could understand in the dream.

It struck Angela that the problem was really between her husband (Terra's father) and his former wife (Terra's mother). Angela realized she was now finished with her part in it!

Terra's father agreed to initiate communication

with Terra's mother to help her understand Angela's position better. Terra's mother became more considerate and understanding of Angela's feelings and needs as a stepmother. Terra became much easier for Angela to deal with, and Angela felt much closer to Terra.

Angela's willingness and love started it all, and the dream helped her begin the process.

As above, so below. In this case, that meant that Angela had an experience in her inner worlds in the dream. This experience seemed to be very real to her and indeed, Terra's mother responded as if she had indeed been a part of Angela's dream.

Making the Connection between Dreams and Our Waking World Can Be a Fun and Interesting Challenge

It's not always easy to see the connections between dreams and your waking life, but if you like a good mystery, it can be quite enjoyable. The greatest game of all is life and its many levels of reality!

Helen wanted a dream to help her with her career change. She didn't ask for this dream consciously, but she had been thinking about being true to herself and finding her mission in life. Her dream seemed complex but made complete sense once she interpreted it.

This was her dream, simplified:

In her friend's living room, a large snake, like a python, had taken up residence under a buffet. Looking more closely, Helen saw that this snake actually

Helen wanted a dream to help her with her career change.

Fearing snakes greatly, Helen kept her distance. Several other people in the room seemed fearless, moving closer to the snake.

What could this dream possibly mean?

had a head that looked like a fish! Fearing snakes greatly, Helen kept her distance. Several other people in the room seemed fearless, moving closer to the snake.

One of the people was named George. He looked like a television sitcom character and also reminded Helen of her stepfather who had the same name. Fearing the snake would bite him, Helen grabbed George and said, "This is the time when it would serve you to be present and to pay attention, or the snake is going to get you!"

All of this time Helen kept her distance, still giving the snake attention from afar. The next time she looked under the buffet there was a lion there with the snake, but she wasn't afraid of the lion. It seemed more like a large cat. The lion then had a baby lion and then turned into a large cat who was very proud of herself for delivering this lion cub.

Helen thought the snake was gone, but its tail was under the cat. It was dying, but George took it outside and gave it a drink with a garden hose.

In the next scene, Helen was with a new friend who was lying on a skateboard, her feet in the air with another skateboard balanced on them. Her friend looked sleek and slim in her new cat suit.

Back in the living room the snake had been revived and was moving toward Helen, who could not get away fast enough. The snake now had hooks like a lobster and hooked Helen's stomach, but there was no pain!

What could this dream possibly mean? Helen decided to write down any history she had that related to anything in the dream. She had a deathly fear of snakes, her stepfather was named George, she related to lions and saw mothers as nurturing. She'd spent the day before having a heart-to-heart conversation with her friend who had been on the skateboard in the dream. Helen especially remembered how the talk with her friend had seemed to change Helen's feeling about her life and its direction.

I asked Helen what some of the symbols meant to her, one by one. They looked like this:

snake = fear
cat = nonconfrontational
George = pathetic
lion mother = nurturing
friend = dream of following her mission
stomach = gut feeling

From these images, Helen determined that this meant the only thing holding her back from her mission was her fear of following her gut feeling. The feeling reminded her of George in the sitcom—wimpy and pathetic. She realized from the dream that she could overcome this feeling by nurturing her life's dream and her instincts, allowing them to come out. She decided she didn't need to confront herself mentally with reasons why it wouldn't work. Trusting herself, and nurturing that trust, was the key.

This busy dream moved Helen in the direction of a new and delightful career. The change was like a breath of fresh air. It helped her take life's adventures to a new, more exciting level. Helen could now accept more of God's gifts in her life.

Trusting herself, and nurturing that trust, was the key.

Some dreams, like Helen's, may seem odd and strange at first, even long and complicated. If you take just one piece of the dream at a time and interpret it, you may get an entire meaning from just that one piece. The "strange" parts may be there just to help you remember an important point. The skateboards meant nothing to Helen, but they made her remember her friend in the dream which connected Helen to the day before and their life-changing conversation.

The dream was a real experience to Helen. It seemed real to her while it was happening, and when she woke up, it still seemed real. She was having an experience on another level of awareness to help her accept the changes she needed to make in her waking life, both in attitude and action. The dream was a powerful, real, and very necessary experience for Helen to move forward in life.

Would you like to have a dream to help you see the connection between the dream world and your waking world? Try the following dream technique for up to thirty days, to see how many of your life experiences begin in your dreams.

Would you like to have a dream to help you see the connection between the dream world and your waking world?

Dream Technique: Above and Below

1. Think of a situation in your life that you would like to understand better.

   Write in your dream journal asking to be given a dream experience you can remember clearly, relating to what's happening in your waking life. And that you would like the dream to come from the highest source of all in your inner worlds.

Example: "I would like a dream to show me the clearest picture of my career challenges right now in my life. I would like this to come from the highest source possible, from the Dream Master, the Mahanta. Please give me a dream I will clearly understand and that will help me see the spiritual view of my situation."

Write this every night for thirty days, if necessary.

2. Write down any dreams you remember.

3. Go through your dream journal once a week, and reread past dreams to see if any may relate to your day-to-day waking life.

Go through your dream journal once a week, and reread past dreams to see if any may relate to your day-to-day waking life.

ANIMALS ARE SOUL TOO, AND YOU CAN MEET THEM IN YOUR DREAMS

Dreams can help us learn more about our lives as Soul (more in chapter 11, "Spiritual Experiences through Dreams") and about animals' lives as Soul too! Animals are Soul too. If you have any doubt about this, read books like *Kinship with All Life* by J. Allen Boone.[6]

Harold Klemp has some astute observations about animals as Soul in his book *The Slow Burning Love of God,* Mahanta Transcripts, Book 13:[7]

"But Soul is Soul.

"There's a higher consciousness growing among people on earth now; they're recognizing this. Scientists are doing studies with monkeys where they seem to have a vocabulary level of a two-year-old. Dogs, in certain cases, seem to have the ability of humans to sense, perceive, and think. And still people say, 'I wonder if they are Soul?'"

Many people have experiences with animals in their dreams. Janet had a dream that helped confirm what she already believed: animals are Soul too. In her dream:

There was a beautiful, full-grown German shepherd with her who was very loving and also very protective. Janet was single and enjoyed traveling alone in her van. She felt this special dog would be a great addition to her family of one. Here was a pet that could not only give her a lot of love but protect her as well. The dog was at her side constantly throughout the dream, vigilant as a sentry, watching for any possible danger.

Janet awoke with a wonderful, peaceful feeling. She hadn't felt this in a very long time. She wondered why. Then suddenly she realized that she had indeed been feeling somewhat uncomfortable about traveling the country alone. Since Janet was very strong and independent, she wouldn't admit to herself that she might need help from anyone or anything. She loved her freedom and rightly so, but wouldn't a pet like this just make it perfect?

A few days after Janet's dream, she was traveling through Arizona. She was on her way to visit

Janet had a dream that helped confirm what she already believed: animals are Soul too.

a friend named David in the beautiful red rock country of northern Arizona. She fell in love with its grandeur as she drove into town. On approach to David's house, a German shepherd puppy came bouncing out from the backyard and jumped all over her, covering her with puppy kisses. She was instantly in love! David came running out of the house, yelling, "Take her, will you? I've got too many mouths to feed as it is!"

"I'd love to!" said Janet, "but you know I am on the road all the time."

"This dog was born to be a nomad. Besides, I had a dream about you two already. I think that Sheba's been looking for you all her life!"

"Well, that clinches it, because I had a dream too!" Janet was so happy and smiling so broadly her mouth hurt.

Sheba and Janet have been happily partnered ever since. It's obvious to Janet that they are loving and dedicated to each other.

Some people say that pets choose their owners. That's true from a Soul perspective (just as we, as Soul, choose our parents). Janet's puppy chose her, as revealed through her and David's dreams. When David and Janet's dreams coincided, it was confirmation for them that their dreams were real experiences for them in their inner worlds.

There are many levels of heaven, and dreams can take place on those many levels. This gives us the opportunity to experience more of life and understand how Divine Spirit works in our everyday life as well. This also helps us understand and be prepared

There are many levels of heaven, and dreams can take place on those many levels. This gives us the opportunity to understand and experience more of life.

for changes that may occur in our waking lives.

In the next chapter a look at prophetic dreams will take us deeper into the many levels of heaven that influence our physical lives.

6

Preparation, or Prophetic, Dreams

Life is a series of interconnected wheels.
Very little can happen to you that isn't known
by you beforehand. All you have to do is learn
to be aware.

—Harold Klemp, *The Dream Master,*
Mahanta Transcripts, Book 8[1]

Life is a series of interconnected wheels. Very little can happen to you that isn't known by you beforehand.

*J*n the Bible, there's a story of a prophetic dream that saved a whole country from famine. Joseph was sold into slavery by his brothers and imprisoned by the pharaoh, but his skill with prophetic dreams saved him from imprisonment and saved the kingdom from starvation. He correctly interpreted the pharaoh's prophetic dream—seven lean cattle devouring the seven fat cattle and seven full ears of corn being eaten by seven withered ears of corn—to mean a seven-year period of crop failures would follow seven years of bountiful harvests.[2]

Many highly respected and creative people throughout history have also had prophetic dreams. Both Charles Dickens and Rudyard Kipling had detailed dreams of future events. Mark Twain dreamed of the death of his younger brother with whom he had been very close.[3]

Large-scale tragic events have been dreamed of in advance by scores of people. Twenty or more reports of precognitive dreams prophesied the sinking of the *Titanic* before its occurrence on April 14, 1912. Twenty-four prophetic dreams were recorded many years later, predicting the disastrous 1966 coal-waste avalanche in Wales where 116 children and 28 adults lost their lives.[4]

Historical war heroes such as Alexander the Great, who had a personal dream interpreter, listened carefully to their dreams to plan war strategies. Julius Caesar had a dream to go forward and led his army across the Rubicon to march against his native Rome and won. However, he lost his life because he didn't listen to his wife's prophetic dream or the soothsayer's warning to "beware the Ides of March." Napoleon kept note of his dreams and used them to plan his campaigns.[5]

Great scientists, philosophers, writers, artists, and musicians have been inspired by prophetic dreams.

Why not tap this source of creativity for yourself?

Volumes could be written about how dreams have shaped our world and have been responsible for abundant amounts of creativity. Why not tap this source of creativity for yourself?

Prophetic Dreams Are Not Just for Prophets

It seems throughout history that if someone had a dream of great significance to mankind, he was called a prophet.

You don't have to be a prophet or famous historical figure to have a prophetic dream, and it doesn't have to be on a grand scale to help you with your future.

How can you tell if a dream is prophetic?

One very simple way to tell is via your intuition—your feelings about the dream. How do you feel when you wake up from a dream about the future that seems very real? Do you feel forewarned? Perhaps you feel an inner knowing that a certain direction may be good for you or not so good for you. The feeling with prophetic dreams is often strong and clear.

Even though the feeling is strong, the meaning of the dream itself might not be obvious. It may be given to you in code. Here's an example.

Sarah traveled by airplane to a seminar far from home. The first night there she dreamed:

She was standing at a clothing rack in a store, and her purse was safely hidden under a stack of clothes so that she could look at the dresses without having to hold it. When she went to look for her purse, it was gone.

Sarah was disturbed by the dream and had a definite feeling of foreboding but thought nothing of it. A few days later she was on her way to the airport to fly home. She had some extra time, so she stopped at the beach with her friend Helen to take a walk. They decided to lock their purses in the car. Helen put her purse under some object to hide it, and Sarah put hers on top of the object.

How can you tell if a dream is prophetic?

When they returned to the car, they found to their dismay that someone had broken into the car. But only Sarah's purse was gone! Sarah realized she'd had a prophetic dream and should have been more careful because of the warning.

Luckily, her friend Helen had extra money and lent some to Sarah for the trip home. Now Sarah is much more responsive to her dreams, especially those she has a strong feeling about!

DREAMS ARE REAL EXPERIENCES IN THE MANY LEVELS OF HEAVEN

The Bible and other holy books, including Eckankar's, speak of different numbered heavens or different levels of heaven. For example, Paul says in the Bible, "I knew a man in Christ above fourteen years ago, (whether in the body, I cannot tell; or whether out of the body, I cannot tell: God knoweth;) such an one caught up to the third heaven."[6] These can also be called higher planes, or more specifically, levels of awareness that are available to us in different ways.

> Dreaming is one way we can explore these higher levels of reality.

Dreaming is one way we can explore these higher levels of reality. In fact, nearly all of your dreams are actual experiences on another plane of life.

It's so exciting to know we can experience heaven now, and one way is through our dreams. Prophetic dreams, or dreams of preparation, are often real experiences on another level of reality. They help us get through experiences here on earth more gracefully.

Sometimes dreams prepare us for a pleasant

experience, so we can accept it fully. A man we will call Gene had a very pleasant prophetic dream that was one of those inner preparations.

Gene's boss handed him an envelope and said to him, "Congratulations on a job well done! Here are two airline tickets so that you and your wife may take a well-earned vacation."

When Gene woke up he felt great but laughed at the thought of his boss giving him a gift like this. That would be the day! Then three months later to the day, his boss thanked him for a job well done and handed him an envelope with tickets and money for a free vacation for him and his wife! The dream had been prophetic and very accurate.

DREAMS HELP US FACE FUTURE EVENTS WITHOUT FEAR

We can experience great fears when we are facing the unknown. Prophetic dreams can help us through these apprehensive times.

A prophetic dream helped one woman through a fearful time. Unlike the dream of the stolen purse, this dream more precisely echoed the event that was to come. It involved a woman we'll call Lori who was about to have a serious operation. Lori was, naturally, quite nervous about her surgery and needed reassurance that no one could truthfully give her.

Lori asked God to help her with this. That night she had a dream that:

She was in the operating room, but she was floating above the table as Soul, looking down on the

We can experience great fears when we are facing the unknown. Prophetic dreams can help us through these apprehensive times.

operating team who were standing over a woman's body. The body was hers! She saw the entire operation going smoothly, hearing positive comments from the surgeon about her very high chances of a good recovery. More important, she felt a tremendous sense of love. She knew then she would be well taken care of.

Next she was in her hospital room, again in her Soul body, talking with the doctor. She could hear the doctor say, "I thought you would recover well, but I had no idea it would be this quickly! You must have someone upstairs working overtime for you."

Lori woke up from the dream feeling much better about checking in to the hospital, realizing she might even be able to do it without shaking with fear. Her operation went very well, and she awoke in her hospital room feeling good about everything. The love was there too, as her family and friends gathered around her and helped in every department of her life.

A few days later the doctor was visiting, and the conversation happened just exactly as it had in her dream! Her prophetic dream helped her in a way that nothing else could.

Here's a technique you can do when you would like to have a prophetic dream to help you through a fearful, anxious, or challenging time.

A few days later the doctor was visiting, and the conversation happened just exactly as it had in her dream!

Dream Technique: How to Have a Prophetic Dream

Since you are Soul, you have a view of the past and future—when your view is not screened by the mind, emotions, and physical events. You can use the dream state to get beyond these temporary limitations.

1. As you are lying in bed with your eyes closed, ready for sleep, imagine you are sitting next to the Dream Master in a lovely outdoor setting. He could be holding your hand, showing you a river that flows by the bench where you are seated.

    The river is the River of Time. All events—past, present, and future—are flowing down this river.

2. Ask the Dream Master to show you the future event or change you're concerned about in your dream. Ask to know how it will all turn out, how you can best handle the situation, or whatever your question is. You may want to bathe in the river, to look for gifts the river might give you to open your awareness more to your dream.

    Sometimes I ask, "Show me the love." This way, if it's an event I'm concerned about, I may be able to see the love in it and the lessons to be learned.

    Feel free to change the recipe in any dream exercise to suit your own tastes, philosophy, beliefs, etc.

3. Write in your dream journal any feelings, words, or images as you awaken. Then contemplate on their significance in relation to your upcoming event or change.

Ask the Dream Master to show you the future event or change you're concerned about in your dream.

Prophetic Dreams Can
Prepare Us for Unexpected Change

Life can take on a dreamlike quality when there are changes about to occur. Perhaps you'd like to see everything from above, like a soaring falcon. Prophetic dreams can help us gain this mountaintop viewpoint. They help us see more clearly, because we're in a state of pure knowing as Soul. Soul knows and uses prophetic dreams as a gift to get past the censor so we may hear the Voice of God.

Soul knows and uses prophetic dreams as a gift to get past the censor so we may hear the Voice of God.

It would be great to know where to go and what to do in life based on this higher awareness. Prophetic dreams can help us gain that awareness to help us through life's changes.

One example: Nancy was excited to be pregnant for the third time and was being very careful with her health because she had previously had two miscarriages. She felt that this pregnancy might finally work, but a dream warned her otherwise:

Nancy was in the hospital, giving birth to her daughter, but she did not see the baby. In the next scene, a nurse walked into Nancy's recovery room looking very distraught. "We've looked everywhere and we just can't seem to find your baby. I'm so sorry you never had a chance to meet her!"

Nancy woke up from the dream in tears. She was so afraid to face the truth she knew the dream was giving her, that she would not be able to carry this baby to full term.

Finally surrendering the situation to God, Nancy felt sure that somehow all would be well, even if she could not have this baby.

Once she decided to face the possibility of this potential change, Nancy and her husband took steps to adopt. After her miscarriage, the couple became happy parents of an adorable six-month-old baby who needed them as much as they needed him. About a year later, Nancy got pregnant and gave birth to a healthy baby, making all her dreams come true!

Handling change can be an incredible challenge, and dreams can help. An Eckankar book I'd recommend to assist with change is *How to Master Change in Your Life: Sixty-seven Ways to Handle Life's Toughest Moments,*[7] by Mary Carroll Moore.

> Handling change can be an incredible challenge, and dreams can help.

LISTENING TO OUR DREAMS MAY TAKE TIME

It's difficult to listen to any type of guidance if we're not ready to take action. Harry had a very striking prophetic dream. He'd been having recurring dreams about marrying women with blond hair. The face of the woman may have been different, but her hair was always blond. In one dream:

Harry was walking in a shopping mall, and he met a woman with blond hair. This time he saw her face clearly.

Believing he would never really meet this person, Harry promptly dismissed the experience but didn't forget the woman's face. Several weeks later he met a woman who looked exactly like the woman in his dream. Harry was very surprised; he got away as fast as he could. He realized he was definitely not interested in marriage yet!

Other people have dreamed about someone they would meet in the future.

How can this be?

You may be having a real experience in the heavenly worlds while your physical body sleeps.

It's the spiritual law: As above, so below. You may be having a real experience in the heavenly worlds while your physical body sleeps. I had such an experience with my husband before I had any idea he was to be my husband.

I was trying Katy's technique, mentioned in the previous chapter. Like her, I'd made a commitment to myself to do whatever it took to create the highest and best possible marriage for me in this lifetime. I decided to begin a journal as Katy had and work with my dreams. I asked to be shown how I could recognize my mate. In a prophetic dream very soon after this:

I was sitting with a man at a baseball game. The couple behind us was talking about vitamin supplements. I turned to them and said, "My husband can help you with that, he's a ———" I named some kind of health professional, like a chiropractor, but I did not feel he was a chiropractor. I gave them one of his business cards, and we returned to enjoying the game.

After having this dream I looked into the eyes of every single male health professional I met, asking the question inwardly, "Are you the one?" No one seemed to fit the bill.

In the meantime, I did a lot of therapy and inner healing with my dreams as well. I let go of a lot of anger, forgave myself, and released old pain.

A close friend in whom I had confided my dream said she knew a couple of single chiropractors in her new place of residence that she wanted me to meet. It never happened. It didn't need to.

About four months later I ran into an old friend at an Eckankar seminar. He and I had both known, because of different dreams, we were going to meet our mates at that seminar in San Francisco.

We just clicked. When we realized there was something special between us, it surprised us at first, then made total sense. I found out he was now an acupuncturist, very strong in the area of nutrition. Just as my dream of the baseball game had shown!

Later, I looked back at my dream journal and found many dreams that prophesied connecting with this particular Soul. We felt it was truly a marriage made in heaven, because it happened first in our dreams. We've learned so much from each other, helping each other to move forward spiritually, and have been working together on many projects we hope will be of service.

A HIGHER COURT SPEAKS

A newly married couple was very concerned about some debts from the husband's previous marriage, and they struggled for over a year to pay these debts. They were both trying to be responsible, yet there were many things they and their children really needed. How could they resolve this issue? Through their spiritual guidance, they decided that bankruptcy was the best option, paying the debts later when they were able to. Though it was a very difficult decision, there seemed no other way, and a higher court seemed to be handing them a clean judgment.

Later, I looked back at my dream journal and found many dreams that prophesied connecting with this particular Soul.

As they prepared to go to bankruptcy court, they felt lighter in some ways, yet there was a heaviness and fear about the proceedings. How would they feel later about all of this? What if they were turned down? What should they wear to make the best impression in court?

The night before their appointment before the judge, the wife was very nervous. She decided to use her dreams and asked for inner guidance to help her through this stressful time. That night she dreamed:

She was in the courtroom, wearing a blue suit she owned, and smiling at the judge. He seemed kind and gentle. The judge decided they were legally deserving of the bankruptcy and said, "I wish you better luck in the future."

She awoke feeling much more comfortable about the entire process. After telling him about the dream, she said to her husband, "I even know what to wear!" They went to court and were pleasantly surprised that the session went just like the dream had prophesied. The judge even said, "I wish you better luck in the future."

The couple has continued to prosper and experience the love of God in their lives, trusting their inner guide, the Mahanta, and continuing to work with their dreams.

You can ask for a specific prophetic dream.

WOULD YOU LIKE TO BE ABLE TO HAVE A PROPHETIC DREAM?

You can ask for a specific prophetic dream just like the woman in the story above. Perhaps there is something specific going on in your life, like a job change, and you want to know in what direction you're headed.

If it's something you can know without interference in your spiritual unfoldment or lessons in life, you may have a dream that will help you see the bigger picture. Keep trying the following exercise until you get some results. Try it with different questions if one doesn't work.

Prophetic dreams usually follow two rules: Your request should be only for yourself, and you need to stay silent about it to let it manifest. I have found it nearly always best to keep these new ideas, projects, or precious thoughts to myself. The energy, force, or desire surrounding a new project or idea is tender like a tiny seedling and can be trampled easily if exposed before its time.

There is a universal spiritual law called the Law of Silence. It can apply to many situations, but in terms of future events, Divine Spirit entrusts us with future knowledge only if we are able to hold it sacred. After all, telling others may influence you subconsciously. Their spoken or unspoken response, even their body language, is picked up subconsciously. Thoughts are very real in the spiritual worlds, and others' thoughts about you or your future can affect the outcome.

Ready to try this special technique? You don't have to wait until bedtime; you can begin step 1 right away.

Prophetic dreams usually follow two rules: Your request should be only for yourself, and you need to stay silent about it to let it manifest.

**Dream Technique: Preparing for
the Future**

1. Think of a specific question about your future. Translate it into a dream request, such as, "Please give me a dream telling me what kind of job I will be getting."

2. As you fall asleep, imagine a temple of any design you would like. Your temple can be any shape, color, or material you can imagine. Ask the Dream Master to guide you to the Golden Wisdom Temple that will best help you to find your answer.

    Then say, "Thy will be done." Surrender your question to the Dream Master, God, or your spiritual guide, as you drift off to sleep.

3. When you awaken, even in the middle of the night, be sure to write down anything that you remember thinking, seeing inwardly, or feeling. Put a reminder of your question on that page of your journal such as, "job dream," then watch what happens!

Surrender your question to the Dream Master, God, or your spiritual guide, as you drift off to sleep.

If you know what the dream means, then it's up to you to take appropriate action, if there is any to take. For instance, if you asked about a job and you kept dreaming you were on the ocean, your course of action might be going to the library to explore jobs that relate to the ocean, such as oceanography, the navy, or a job on a cruise ship. Maybe your new job will have to do with food from the sea. You know best.

Prophetic dreams can help us realize that our lives can be explored more fully than we've ever imagined. Be careful to use these talents only for yourself.

CIRCUMSTANCES AND CONDITIONS CHANGE AS YOUR CONSCIOUSNESS CHANGES

Whatever direction you're headed in at this moment, it's affected by the attitudes, beliefs, or opinions you have right now. When a dream shows you a possible future situation you don't like, you can take charge of your future by changing the attitudes and opinions you have surrounding it. In essence, this is changing your consciousness. For example, years ago when I was single and very lonely, I kept having dreams and intuitive feelings that I would never be married again and would probably spend the rest of my life alone. This did not sit well with me at all! I decided to try changing my attitudes about it.

I opened myself to the Holy Spirit, or the ECK as we say in Eckankar, and asked for help. The love of God began to unravel old attitudes and beliefs based on patterns from my childhood and many past lives. Over several years the healing took place as I struggled to overcome my fears of isolation and loneliness.

The love of God began to unravel old attitudes and beliefs based on patterns from my childhood and many past lives.

Eventually, I learned to love myself more and be happier on my own. With help from the Mahanta, the Dream Master, and my spiritual exercises, my consciousness changed and I was able to meet my husband. It was as though I had created a whole new lifetime for myself!

You can change many prophesies you may not like by simply changing how you view life.

You can change many prophesies you may not like by simply changing how you view life. If you are open to changing the attitudes that may cause the future condition to occur, you can change those conditions.

Now that we've covered the future, what about the past? What about lifetimes that may haunt us in our dreams without our even knowing what they are? Many of life's problems can be traced back to a past life, as you will see in the next chapter.

7

Past-Life Awareness in Dreams

The study of dreams in Eckankar begins with the fact of past lives. All conditions are due to karma, and some will last a lifetime, such as the loss of a limb. A study of dreams can help people learn the spiritual reason their life is as it is, and what they can do to improve their lot.

—Harold Klemp, *The Art of Spiritual Dreaming*[1]

HAVE YOU LIVED BEFORE?

Would it surprise you to know General George Patton believed in reincarnation? Not only did he believe in it, he remembered many past lives as a warrior—from a Carthaginian soldier dying of thirst to a Viking. Patton also had a strong belief in God.[2]

Soul is a spark of God, eternal and immortal. Bodies are taken on by Soul to experience life in its myriad forms so Soul can expand and grow in Its capacity to love. So as Soul, we journey from life to life, gathering wisdom, learning to give and receive divine love, God's love, through numerous life-forms.

Soul is a spark of God, eternal and immortal.

Doesn't it make sense to you that Soul goes on learning and growing throughout eternity? How can just one lifetime of experience teach Soul all the lessons It needs to learn? After all, on earth alone there are so many cultures, societies, personalities, bodies, careers, art forms, and educational opportunities. And let's not forget, two completely different sexes (and if you've ever lived or worked with the opposite sex, you know how different men and women can be, as hard as we try to be balanced!).

Have you noticed there are certain people you meet who you could swear you have met before? Have you visited a place for the first time and found it very familiar? Perhaps you've been with this person or lived in this place during a past life.

When a child comes into the world, looking and acting like his or her great grandmother, you might ask the child (at about three or four years old) something like, "What did you do when you were big, like me?" Get ready for some very surprising answers. You may even want to take notes! It may be that the child is talking about several lifetimes back. One three-year-old I visited was strumming a guitar loudly, albeit off-key, and singing a tune he was making up as he went along. Impressed by his stage presence, I asked him what he used to do when he was big. He said, "I used to play and sing for people." I thought to myself, *Gee, I wonder if we've finally found Elvis?*

We are mercifully blind to our past lives until we're ready to take responsibility for them.

DREAMS ARE A DOORWAY TO PAST LIVES

We are mercifully blind to our past lives until we're ready to take responsibility for them. There are those lives in which we've made major blunders and some for which we may take too much credit.

Why would we want to know about our past lives (especially if they were unhappy or painful)? Past-life recall can help us resolve problems today. It may give us the insight to understand fears, illnesses, financial loss, relationship issues, and more. Nearly every unfounded fear in this lifetime comes from a past life. Fear of heights, fear of drowning, fear of flying in airplanes or riding trains can often be traced to a catastrophe or death in a past life. Dreams can help us explore past-life traumas that may be causing fear and stress in this life.

> Past-life recall can help us resolve problems today.

John is a former bodyguard and holds a black belt in two forms of martial arts. Yet with all his strength and courage, he had a fear of flying in airplanes. His mother worked for an airline, so his family flew free when he was a child. Every few months, the family took off for adventures to a different state or country. John did fine until he grew up, got engaged, and prepared to settle down. Then, every time he took an airplane ride, he felt shaky inside. He would close his eyes upon takeoff and landing, afraid to even look out the window. He was especially frightened during turbulence.

What had changed since his childhood? He couldn't figure it out until one day he had this dream:

John was copilot in a World War II fighter plane. Without warning, John felt a blasting wind in his face as the plane dove, out of control. They'd been hit!

He knew in that moment that his life was over. Just before the plane hit the ground—

John woke up in a cold sweat. The shock he felt from the impending crash was real, yet here he lay in his bed, where he was usually quite comfortable! Deciding it was just his mind working overtime, John went on with his life. But he was still afraid of flying. One day he asked the Dream Master, the Mahanta, whom he looks to for help in his dreams, to help him see the truth of the situation. Here's the dream he had next:

A big band of the World-War-II era was playing the dance tune, "In the Mood." Everyone, including John, was on the USO dance floor, swinging to the hippest beat in history. With his soon-to-be wife in his arms, he was waiting for his call to duty so he could serve his country, come home, and spend the rest of his life with her. Right in midswing, the door to the dance hall flew open. A sergeant from the army yelled, "It's time boys, we've been called to defend our country. We leave in just two hours! Get packed and ready to go NOW!"

John and his fiancée, Laura, shared a swift good-bye kiss, and he was off to war. Somehow, he knew he would never return.

The next scene was the same as in his previous dream. He faced the same fear of death as his plane began to plunge, but he also felt an overpowering sadness. He would never see his Laura again.

John woke from this dream with a strong feeling of loss. This loss overshadowed the fear of death from

> John went on with his life. But he was still afraid of flying. One day he asked the Dream Master, the Mahanta, whom he looks to for help in his dreams, to help him see the truth of the situation.

the first dream. Somehow, he knew this wasn't just a dream but a real experience he'd had in a former life. The key to that realization was the intense feeling of sadness.

When he was first dating his fiancée in this life, she became hesitant to get too involved too soon. He said, "I just don't want to lose you again!" How foolish that sounded, but it felt absolutely right. When he told her about his dreams, she confirmed her memories of that lifetime as well. Every time she heard big-band music lately, she wanted to cry.

Now it all made perfect sense! His present fiancée was also his fiancée in that past life, Laura. The truth filled him with such happiness. Now they could be together again! Now John is not nearly so afraid to fly. Though a bit of the old shakiness still lingers, it's dissipating gradually over time.

Would you like to resolve some issues that may relate to past lives? In his book *A Modern Prophet Answers Your Key Questions about Life,*[3] Harold Klemp says about past lives and dreams:

> Would you like to resolve some issues that may relate to past lives?

"It is easiest to trace past lives through a study of your dreams.

"To awaken such past-life dreams, make a note of things you greatly like or dislike. Do that also with people. Then watch your dreams. Also note if a certain country or century attracts you. There is a reason."

Try the dream technique to follow for help with resolving past-life issues. If your desire is to unfold spiritually, solve everyday fears or problems, or improve your life, this can help. Make sure you give plenty of time for your mind to accept this. It may mean thirty to ninety days of dedication to this technique. If it still doesn't work for you, try it again in a year or whenever you feel so inclined.

For the sake of clarity, I'd recommend working with just one issue at a time until you resolve it or at least get a good handle on it. Sometimes you get a bonus when your dreams or past-life recalls reveal answers to your other questions at the same time.

Dream Technique: Past-Life Help for Present-Life Challenges

1. Choose one issue you'd like to resolve through past-life awareness. Ask for help from the Dream Master or God. Write down your unexplained fear, issue, or health concern.

2. As you go to sleep, think about how this problem makes you feel. Let any images that come into your mind just be there. As you're allowing yourself to experience these old feelings and thoughts, imagine tossing them all into a large film canister that the Dream Master is holding. Ask him to make a movie for you from the lifetime these feelings began in.

3. When you wake up, write down any dreams you remember, no matter how crazy they seem to you.

4. Ask yourself how these dreams may relate to your present-day problem if the dreams were actually of a past life.

As you're allowing yourself to experience these old feelings and thoughts, imagine tossing them all into a large film canister that the Dream Master is holding.

Past-life recall in dreams or in waking life can help us to get past blocks that may be holding us back in any area of life. Sam had a dream that helped him understand why he had a strong fear of writing. Even though he loved writing, he'd done little of it because some nameless shadow within him was holding him back. He couldn't quite describe it when you asked him. Then Sam had a dream that covered several lifetimes and helped him to identify the shadow.

Sam was walking down a narrow hallway in his dream as quickly as he could without attracting too much attention. He was hoping no one would stop him to ask what was in his leather satchel. It seemed a dark and dreary time in history, with very little public knowledge of the real intent of government and church united. Sam had been writing essays on this "power out of control" situation, signing them "The Hound," and he knew he could be hanged at any minute, if he were caught.

Next, he was leaning over a table, writing by dim candlelight. He was in another life. This time he was bold enough to be helping others translate the Bible into English. His work had to be done in secret, as there were groups who would kill him the moment they knew of his nightly writing ritual.

A third scene, unrelated to the rest, found Sam dressed in solicitor's (English attorney's) clothing. He was, again, wary of anyone who knew what he was writing. This time, Sam was warning the layperson of how the law really worked in England at that time. The peasants were the underdogs, and Sam was there to help, as usual, with the written word.

Past-life recall in dreams or in waking life can help us to get past blocks that may be holding us back in any area of life.

Waking from
this very long
dream, Sam
knew without a
doubt that
these were
recollections of
past lives.

Waking from this very long dream, Sam knew without a doubt that these were recollections of past lives. They were real scenes to him. As Soul, he knew this with certainty. Because of this awareness, he gradually understood why he'd always felt this seemingly unfounded fear of writing. He realized his fear of chastisement—or worse, death—held him back subconsciously.

Sam couldn't understand his fears about writing until he had this dream of past lives. They showed him why he had fear and resistance to expressing himself through the written word. What freedom to finally know! It took time for him to overcome his past-life conditioning to writing in secret, but he worked on getting past the fear. Sam's awareness put him in control of the fear, and he's begun writing regularly!

A past-life dream helped me understand an unusual fear I had as a little girl. We were not very well-to-do, and yet I had rich relatives. One uncle seemed to treat people like he owned them. I felt I had to do whatever he said.

Because of the irritation I felt from this uncle, I told my father, "I never want to be rich." I remember him saying to me, "Don't ever say that!" But he never asked me why I was so dead set against it. I respected my father's wishes and never said it to him again. Yet somehow it became such a part of me that I could never seem to get ahead financially.

What was holding me back from being financially stable, with a savings account like most people? I knew how to support myself and could make good money, but it slipped through my fingers like fine sand. No matter how much discipline I used to save money, some unexpected need, like car repairs, would come along, and there would go my nest egg. I decided it was time to get to the bottom of all this. I asked for a dream that would show me what I needed to see. What was holding me back from being more financially stable? Here's what I dreamed:

I was wealthy beyond measure, a monarch ruling a tiny kingdom yet keeping all the wealth to myself. I had other faults, but this one reflected the power I held and used to control my subjects. They would have only what was needed and nothing more. The rest would be paid in taxes to me, the king. I looked upon them as children—or worse, people I owned in some way. In my estimation they were there to serve me and serve me they would.

I woke up from that dream horrified. Could that have been me playing the role of power-hungry king? It felt like me, since I was having the dream. However, I simply could not relate to this experience and was unwilling to claim it as one of my lives. I wrote the dream in my journal and went about my life.

The following week I was reading over my dream journal and came across the dream again, noticing the question I 'd written just before it: "Dear Dream Master, please help me to know what blocks are in the way of financial stability for me. Please give me a dream that will help me to understand in a way I can see and interpret clearly." Just then, I realized

I asked for a dream that would show me what I needed to see. What was holding me back from being more financially stable?

the dream I'd just had was the clearest message I could have gotten. I was just too focused on being spiritual this lifetime to believe I could have been so negative and cruel.

Though difficult to face, this dream helped me realize I was just paying back for the misery I'd caused in past lives. Even though we do these terrible things, we still live and breathe to see a fruitful, loving tomorrow. Life has a way of balancing itself. When we've learned the lesson, we can move on. Some religions call this karma. It has certainly become a popular term and explains so many of life's mysteries.

It's not easy to face, but once we have begun to explore the notion of past lives, we begin to see that we were not always good or kind. After all, we're here on earth to learn, and making mistakes is a natural part of that process. That royal-scoundrel lifetime was one of my bigger blunders, but there were probably a lot more, most that I may never need to know about (thank heaven!).

The lifetimes I wish to explore are ones that will help me find the secret keys to difficult problems. These may have me locked in certain attitudes, beliefs, fears, or views of life and keep me blinded to greater love and awareness.

One big fear I had in the past was the fear of finding out about unpleasant lifetimes: lifetimes where I was a victim of some horrible deed or where I was the perpetrator. Either discovery could be upsetting. How was I to deal with these emotions?

Life has a way of balancing itself. When we've learned the lesson, we can move on.

BEING CHILDLIKE HELPS TO
GET THROUGH PAST-LIFE RECALLS

How does one face the possibility of unpleasant past lives while attempting to resolve this life's issues? I've learned from Eckankar simply to look at myself as a spiritual child and the world as a school with a big playground. The Dream Master, the Mahanta, is my teacher. If I listen to his inner instruction, all will be well. That doesn't mean it will always be pleasant, but the love and protection is always there. I know that anything I experience in this life is a necessary part of my schooling as Soul. I also know that trusting this process is the only way I can maintain my sense of balance and harmony in life.

The playground is where I can practice building sand castles. Some will stay up, and some will fall down. The only way I learn to build better is by practice. A childlike attitude of exploration and experimentation helps me feel less guilt.

Karma, as mentioned before, is life's way of teaching us more about following the spiritual laws to create a life filled with love and freedom. It's easy to feel guilty when we're reminded by life that we have broken one of its laws, such as not interfering in another's space (the Law of Noninterference) or keeping our agreements (the Law of Karma).

However, feeling guilty is not the means to pay for past mistakes. Guilt makes us aware we've done something we need to correct. Other than that, feeling guilty is fairly useless.

Being human, it's difficult not to feel a range of emotions from sadness to guilt to a drop in self-esteem

How does one face the possibility of unpleasant past lives while attempting to resolve this life's issues?

about one action or another. My saving grace is to ask myself, "Did you learn anything from it?" If I can say yes, I'm a step ahead. If not, I need to look more closely at the gift of wisdom for me in the experience. Dreams can help us get through this too. Just ask for help with these emotions in the dream state.

My saving grace is to ask myself, "Did you learn anything from it?"

Here's one more story of a past-life recall which helped someone understand her present-life relationship with her partner: Hilda had difficulty trusting that her husband, George, would be there to support her and love her throughout their lives. He was dedicated to her, and Hilda knew that. Why the worry?

Hilda went to see a therapist who told her she must have some childhood issue that caused her to feel this way, as George had never given her a reason. Hilda told the therapist she remembered a lovely childhood with strict, but loving parents. They never gave her any reason to feel abandoned. Her parents got along just fine.

The therapist was insistent that something must have happened to cause Hilda to feel as she did. Hilda left the counselor's office feeling confused and disturbed. She later asked her parents and other relatives about her younger years. They all told her the same thing. Her parents were strict disciplinarians but always gave her love. They loved each other very much. There simply wasn't anything else to tell her, except about the small spats every couple has.

Hilda decided to try a dream technique a friend had given her. *It might help,* she thought. Her dream that night was full, very real, and very emotional:

Hilda was walking through a park in the early morning, while it was still dark. She was dressed too lightly for the cool weather. She felt afraid and hungry, all at the same time. Talking to herself like someone a little crazy, Hilda said, "If only he hadn't gone, if only he were still here!" Stopping by a bakery, she smelled the bread being baked for the day and almost fainted with hunger from its sweet aroma. She forced herself to walk on. Looking for odd jobs, she seemed unable to find work and decided to walk to the next town, which was very far away.

It began to snow, lovely perfect flakes that sparkled in the rising sun. However, Hilda became very cold and, because she was hungry, could simply go no further. She sat under a great oak tree, feeling absolutely no reason to live. She froze to death. She saw her body as she floated away from it and said to herself, "Now I can have peace."

Hilda was dreaming about her past life with George, in which he had gone off to war. No one in the small European town helped her because she followed a different religion than everyone else in the village. George had married her against his parents' wishes, but they were very much in love, so they simply stayed very much to themselves.

When George was ordered into the service and soon became missing in action, Hilda had no way to earn a living for herself. Now she understood her great fear of George leaving in this life. Hilda knew the lesson for her in this life was to find a way to be independent and responsible for herself. She needed to be able to support herself so that if something

Hilda knew the lesson for her in this life was to find a way to be independent and responsible for herself.

did happen to him again, she would feel like she could survive. Hilda realized the spiritual quality of freedom comes with self-responsibility.

The study of past lives can be a blessing when it assists us in moving forward both spiritually and in our everyday lives.

For a deeper study of past lives, the Eckankar books are very informative, especially Linda Anderson's *35 Golden Keys to Who You Are & Why You're Here,*[4] mentioned earlier in this book.

Opening up to your past lives may help you resolve nightmares and recurring dreams. The next chapter gives you more tools to work with those unwelcome dreams.

The study of past lives can assist us in moving forward both spiritually and in our everyday lives.

8

Recurring Dreams, Dreams of Intrusion, and Nightmares

Negative experiences are the testing ground of Soul. They are there purposely for you to overcome. The Dream Master can overcome some nightmares for you, but he may not always take care of the entire nightmare. In some instances, you may be facing a karmic debt that you created many years ago. It is better to work it out in the dream state than to have this karmic debt appear in your physical life.

—Harold Klemp, *The Dream Master,*
Mahanta Transcripts, Book 8[1]

Negative experiences are the testing ground of Soul.

WHY DO WE HAVE UNPLEASANT DREAMS?

Why do we have unpleasant, upsetting, or traumatic dreams? We could just as easily ask, Why do people have unpleasant experiences in everyday life? The answers to both questions may be the same: to learn a tough lesson, face fears from the past, resolve past karma, or simply become more aware of something we've been avoiding in ourselves.

The ego wants to be comfortable and feel good about itself while Soul, the higher self, just wants to unfold spiritually. Soul may create these experiences if It's not getting through to our minds any other way. When we suffer, our hearts are softened by the experience and we gain more compassion for others. So in this way, dreams of an intense nature may even open our hearts more.

On the other hand, if something disturbing happens in our dreams, it may be the intrusion of someone else's thoughts or feelings. This chapter will give you tools to protect yourself.

Recurring dreams could be inner experiences preparing you for a new cycle. They may be helping you resolve past-life karma or pushing you to accept a new level of awareness. However, they may be disturbing if they're about fearful experiences, such as the following:

> *June was being chased by ghosts, or at least she thought they were ghosts. Since she never turned around to see who was chasing her, she didn't really know what it was! She did feel she was in a haunted house and therefore assumed her pursuers were without bodily form. She ran and ran and finally felt herself falling.*

June had been having the above dream for years. She always woke up just as she was falling, in a cold sweat, her heart racing as if she'd really been running, fearful of being caught by her pursuers. June asked me what I thought it meant. I told her she was the only one who could really know. I also mentioned

Recurring dreams could be inner experiences preparing you for a new cycle.

I knew a technique for changing the dream or perhaps learning more about her pursuers.

I called June later on to ask if the technique worked and what she had decided her dream meant. She told me the technique was successful and that she realized her pursuers represented her own fears.

The following dream technique was the one I shared with June. When you're feeling out of control in your dreams, you may want to try this too.

Dream Technique: The Loving Knight

1. As you wake after a disturbing dream, keep your eyes closed for a moment. Think of which part of the dream disturbed you most, whether it was a person, animal, or event.

2. Imagine yourself as a loving knight in shining armor. The armor protects you completely. You have a sword made of pure light, sound, and love. Imagine that it can shoot out a beam of light that would not hurt anyone but simply protect you with love.

   Visualize yourself facing your ghost or adversary, and send out your beam of light and love, knowing it will light up the situation for you and give you more insight about the dream.

3. Tell yourself that the next time you have a dream like this, you will be in control, because now you have a plan and protection! You can use this method while you're dreaming if you are aware in your dream.

> Imagine yourself as a loving knight in shining armor. The armor protects you completely.

> 4. One more important step is to ask for help from the Dream Master, or whoever you look to spiritually to guide you in the heavenly worlds.

Many people have recurring dreams of being chased. Another example is Susan's. She resolved a very frightening recurring dream using love in a unique way.

Large, ugly monsters were pressing in on Susan as she ran for her life. She was desperate for help.

Susan was finally fed up with this dream. What could she do? She decided to use her divine gift of imagination. A wonderful idea struck her even as she was going into another dream about the monsters. She would tell them what beautiful jobs they were doing as monsters and offer herself as a reference if they ever wanted jobs doing what they do best—being monsters! She never had that dream again.

Why not try this technique yourself, and see how it works to befriend or employ your monsters, ghosts, or attackers? This may seem a bit far out when you feel fear. A way to turn that around might be to realize that you are in control. Make yourself the boss of your dreams.

Make yourself the boss of your dreams.

Marie made such a decision, realizing she could be in charge of her dreams and thus resolve a disturbing recurring dream.

She was locked in a basement. It was frightening and frustrating. When would she get out?

Marie had this dream over and over again. She never got out until she woke up. She felt like she was missing some important lesson. Marie decided to imagine her way out. When she woke up she did a spiritual exercise and created a new scenario. Imagining windows in the basement, Marie decided to give them latches she could easily reach to open and climb out!

Marie realized she could take the experience from her dream and apply it to her waking life. Dreams are just another way of experiencing life, she mused, because they're just as real. As above, so below.

Because of that dream, Marie became aware of how often she limited herself. She now knows how to expand herself into new territory and has been breaking limits right and left!

Dreams are a great testing ground to experiment with our spiritual gifts as Marie did. Recurring dreams may help us see that we have a way to overcome fear with love. One aspect of God's love that can help us overcome fear is imagination. We can use our divine gift of imagination to be the positive creators of our lives, authors of our futures.

One more instance of a recurring nightmare was almost humorous. Robert kept having a dream in which:

He was continually fighting, being hit, and hitting another person. The person he fought with was different in each dream.

Robert always won the fight, but it was still a disturbing feeling to have to continually fight in his

One aspect of God's love that can help us overcome fear is imagination.

dreams. When Robert told me about this recurring dream, I asked him what quality he would give each of these people he fought with. He said they all seemed very "resistant." I let him think about that for a while, then he told me that he realized it had to do with his work. Robert told me he felt as though he was constantly fighting with his editors. He was working at the time in the publishing industry and was convinced that his dreams reflected his day-to-day nightmare.

What could he do?

Robert could turn this situation around both in his dreams and his day-to-day life. One suggestion I gave him was to invite the opponent in his dream to a picnic. If he were to imagine a beautiful picnic laid out on a cheerful checkered cloth with lovely wineglasses and delicious food, he could change the whole feeling of the dream. He could visualize a lovely, warm, and picturesque setting for the picnic, asking his antagonist if he or she wouldn't rather have a lovely picnic than fight.

Once he was able to turn the situation in his dreams toward a more positive outcome, Robert's waking life changed as well, and he got along much better with his editors!

> Robert could turn this situation around both in his dreams and his day-to-day life. One suggestion I gave him was to invite the opponent in his dream to a picnic.

NIGHTMARES CAN BE FRIGHTENING, BUT YOU CAN USE THEM TO MOVE FORWARD

What good could come of having nightmares? Like in the recurring dreams above, the dreamer may learn to take charge of his dreams; rely more on love and guidance from the Mahanta, the Dream

Master; and use these tools to create a better waking life as well. Many fears from this life or past lives can be resolved while you sleep.

One article stated that dreams of people who have become blind may help them overcome trauma. The dreams they have may be frightening and bring up many fears for them about being blind, but the dreams also help them become more accepting of their situation. This article called these undoing dreams. The subjects having post-traumatic-shock syndrome seemed to show improvement after having such dreams in which they dreamed a different outcome.[2]

Another article investigated the function of dreams in adaptation to stress over time. After a particularly stressful experience, the dreamers would have negative dreams. These dreams included details of the stressful experiences with the dreamer's attempt to master them. These dreams were called poststress mastery dreams.[3]

Stressful experiences in both instances gave the dreamers the opportunity to gain more mastery over their waking lives. Becoming aware of these opportunities as spiritual experiences have helped many people overcome stressful times even faster.

A case in point was when Daria had a dream that helped her better understand her relationship with her husband. In her dream:

Daria's beautiful cats turned into rats and were crawling all over the bed while she and her husband were sleeping! Daria's husband sat up in bed and inadvertently sat on one of the rats and killed it.

> Many fears from this life or past lives can be resolved while you sleep.

Daria woke up in tears, because the rat in her dream was really her cat, in her mind. She was horrified. However, when she had calmed down and had some time to think about the dream, she realized it had to do with her relationship with her husband. Feeling he sometimes overpowered her with his masculine energy, Daria felt "crushed." Since she loved her cats very much, her subconscious mind only allowed them to be killed as rats, so she wouldn't be too disturbed. Daria told me the cat that was crushed represented her.

Once Daria was able to sort out her emotions and speak with her husband about it, she felt more free in their relationship and within herself. She was able to use her nightmare to her advantage, both personally and spiritually.

Another frightening dream turned out to be a blessing in disguise; it helped Kristen know that she was always protected. She had just seen a very negative and hideous painting a woman had done while feeling vengeful and needing to express it. The painting somehow seeped into Kristen's dream, and she woke up very disturbed by a dream she did not fully remember. She only knew the dream was somehow influenced by her reaction to the painting.

Kristen turned on her light with shaking fingers and asked the Dream Master, the Mahanta, for help. She was newly acquainted with the spiritual leader of Eckankar, whose inner presence she was beginning to feel in her life. She still had doubts about how someone could give her so much unconditional, divine love and be with her always. The love and

The painting somehow seeped into Kristen's dream, and she woke up very disturbed by a dream she did not fully remember. Kristen turned on her light with shaking fingers and asked the Dream Master, the Mahanta, for help.

protection of the Mahanta was something that seemed a little too good to be true.

The shock of the dream motivated her to ask directly for a sign so that she would know that he really was with her. To prove to herself that the Mahanta's protection really was always with her, Kristen asked to hear the song she loved sung by James Taylor, "You've Got a Friend."

The next day Kristen's husband was helping a friend move into a new home. The friend gave Kristen's husband a gift, and he in turn brought it home to Kristen. It was a James Taylor CD. On the label was her favorite song, and the specific sign she was looking for, "You've Got a Friend." She was so grateful to know that her spiritual teacher would always be with her! Even though Kristen's dream was very frightening, it had given her the impetus she needed to ask for the truth with her whole heart and without hesitation. She was grateful, even for this nightmare, because she could see the blessing in it.

Would you like a special technique that has worked for thousands of people to experience more love, protection, and guidance in their dreams? Try this next technique and get ready for some great changes in your dream world and in your life!

Imagine yourself back in the dream with the Dream Master, the Mahanta, by your side. Ask for his help in understanding the dream.

Dream Technique: You've Got a Friend

1. After a nightmare or recurring dream, take some time to contemplate on it. Imagine yourself back in the dream with the Dream Master, the Mahanta, by your side. Ask for his help in understanding the dream.

2. Imagine what might happen differently in the dream, now that you have a powerful friend to protect you and help you see the whole picture.

How might you react differently? What might you see that you did not see before?

3. Ask the Dream Master to be your ally in any future dream that disturbs you. Impress upon yourself that this is exactly what will happen next time you have a dream like this: You will have your dream friend, the Dream Master, by your side.

Ask the Dream Master to be your ally in any future dream that disturbs you.

RECURRING NIGHTMARES MAY OPEN THE WAY TO HEALING

Having had a recurring dream about a glass breaking in my mouth, I found myself wondering, *What on earth could it mean?* It only took me about ten years to get it!

The dream was very frightening as I had no way of knowing that my glass would break as soon as I took a drink of water from it. I felt fear above all.

In looking at this dream and my life, it made no sense to me. Then I used the T-Technique in chapter 2 to interpret this dream. There was one image in the dream—the glass. I knew what it meant to me— fragile. Then it struck me almost immediately that I was the one who was fragile!

I was emotionally frail during that portion of my life, needing love and affection and feeling I had none. The key word here is *feeling*. The love was there, because life gives us all of the love we can receive. When I went to drink from the "cup of life," it would break due to my inability to receive.

Once I learned how to give myself this love and accept it from all life around me, I no longer had that upsetting dream.

I was grateful to have had that recurring dream to open the way for the healing to occur. Over time, I became stronger and stronger emotionally.

In many dreams, parts of us may be represented by nearly every image we see. When we're honest with ourselves, we can bring about great healing. Again, this may take some time, so give yourself a lot of love and patience with the process. After all, we're here to learn, so why not make the most of it?

A man we'll call Max had a spiritual awakening stemming from a nightmare he had as a child. In this recurring dream:

Young Max found himself in a certain house. He knew if he went to a specific closet in that house he would see a skeleton inside. The skeleton might move slightly or not. Even though he thought to himself, I should be afraid, *he felt no fear, just curiosity.*

Years later after Max grew up, he realized that he was truly unafraid while he was in that dream. This understanding came to him when he found the teachings of Eckankar and discovered that Soul is eternal and that he could visit heaven in this lifetime. The dream made sense now. He was no longer confused about his lack of fear regarding a representative of

> In many dreams, parts of us may be represented by nearly every image we see.

death, the skeleton. To Max, the skeleton represented the most basic bit of knowledge he had as a child regarding death.

Even as a child, Max was not afraid of his body dying. He had always known subconsciously there was more to life beyond the veil of death and was curious about what was there! Now he knows for sure, as he travels beyond his body daily in his spiritual exercises.

WHAT ARE DREAMS OF INTRUSION?

Dreams of intrusion occur when we are open to someone who may have an agenda with which we've not consciously agreed. Subconsciously we may not know how to close the inner door to that person's strong emotions or personality.

For example, if newly divorced parents disagree on visiting rights, one parent may try to influence the other in the dream state, without either party being aware of it.

All of this happens on a subconscious level, but the good news is, it's another opportunity to develop spiritual awareness, strength, and stamina.

WHAT COULD BE THE PURPOSE FOR DREAMS OF INTRUSION?

Perhaps the purpose for dreams of intrusion is to help us better know where our space ends and another person's begins. Knowing ourselves is part of spiritual unfoldment. We must know ourselves before we can know God.

The path back home to God is such a rocky one,

> Dreams of intrusion occur when we are open to someone who may have an agenda with which we've not consciously agreed.

but I've found that every single rock has a purpose. It helps when I stop to be aware of the purpose of the rock rather than cursing it. When I'm lucky, I catch myself before I've tripped over too many! This is illustrated by a dream I had for many years:

I was being pursued by someone I wasn't feeling good about, yet I found myself attracted to him. I felt as though I could not resist his advances and became more and more entangled in a web of passion that felt like it wasn't my own.

These dreams were mine and yet they were not mine. I was so in need of love at the time, as illustrated in the dream about the breaking glass, that I was too open to anyone who came along. Even when I knew deep down inside that someone wasn't right for me in my waking life, I would go ahead and get to know him better. The desperate, lonely part of me hoped he'd reveal some wonderful hidden traits or suddenly turn into the "right" person, like in the fairy tale where a frog turns into a prince!

Because I was so in need of love, I was open in my dream state as well. The situation was not healthy, not what I wanted. There were men coming into my dream state who would never have interested me in waking life.

Once I realized what was happening, I became more aware of being too open to anything and learned to get more love from within myself.

A different kind of dream of intrusion can occur when someone wants you to do something you'd rather not. Perhaps it's a boss or business competitor. Maybe

Once I realized what was happening, I became more aware of being too open to anything and learned to get more love from within myself.

it's even your child or mate. David had a dream that began innocently enough:

While fishing early one morning at his favorite spot in the river, David rested and relaxed as the sun rose higher, shedding golden light everywhere. The water in the river shone and began to ripple slightly. The ripples became bigger and bigger, sending floods of water over the shore and over David! A strong wind picked up and tossed him away from the river, onto dry land.

David woke up feeling disturbed, even a bit angry. He loved to go fishing in his waking life and was planning on doing so the next day. He wondered how this dream could have been his. It simply didn't seem to fit any of his own images or feelings about fishing. He tried interpreting it as a dream of his own, wondering what it could possibly mean. He kept thinking about the feeling of anger that didn't seem to be his. Disappointment that his fishing trip was ruined in the dream would have certainly made sense, but not anger. It just didn't add up.

The only thing that kept coming back into David's mind he rejected as being silly. The thought was that his wife simply didn't like the time he spent fishing and wanted more attention for herself. *Why, she's never said anything!* thought David. Still, he realized he needed to clarify the situation with his wife and help her understand that it was an important time for him to get more in tune with Divine Spirit and with himself. This time alone helped him to be a more balanced person and therefore easier to live with!

> He wondered how this dream could have been his. It simply didn't seem to fit any of his own images or feelings about fishing.

He decided he would let her know he loved her very much and would set aside more time to spend with her as well, time she could count on every week.

Once David spoke with his wife and realized she indeed was feeling neglected, he knew the dream was a reflection of her feelings which she didn't have the courage to tell him about directly.

When you find others doing something in your dreams they would be very unlikely to do in your waking life, be aware that it may not really be the person you think it is. For example, here's a story that illustrates this point.

In waking life Jim is Colette's boss. In Colette's dream he appears to be the same person, Jim, her boss, but he is acting very out of character. In the dream:

Jim tells Colette he has accepted the offer another company made to take over a small subsidiary which Colette now manages.

In waking life, Jim was happy with Colette's progress with this subsidiary so far. He had told her to stay with it for about five more years, growing the company to the point where it would be easy to sell for ten million dollars, if they chose to let it go. Just recently, a Fortune 500 company had recognized the growth potential of this small offshoot and wanted the profits for itself. An offer of two million dollars was made by a very aggressive individual who wouldn't seem to take no for an answer. Every trick in the book had been tried, but Jim held fast, promising Colette this sale would not go through for several years at least, if then.

> When you find others doing something in your dreams they would be very unlikely to do in your waking life, be aware that it may not really be the person you think it is.

Who could be masquerading as Jim in this dream? Perhaps the aggressive negotiator for the Fortune 500 company, or maybe his boss. Likely it was someone involved in this potentially hostile takeover. What would you do in this type of dream situation? The following technique may help.

Dream Technique: Eliminating Intruders

1. Ask the Dream Master, the Mahanta, or your own spiritual guide for spiritual guidance and protection in your dreams and waking life as well.

2. Imagine surrounding yourself with light and love before you go to sleep.

3. Order the intruder out of your space, and do not associate with him, if at all possible.

Imagine surrounding yourself with light and love before you go to sleep.

The last step in this dream technique may be especially necessary if your dream intruder is emotionally unbalanced. If necessary, change your phone number, address, or anything you need to do to maintain your privacy in your life and in your dreams.

Even balanced people can have a difficult time with control. Controlling oneself is necessary, but attempts to control others can backfire. The person who is trying to control you will certainly meet their own lessons along the way. In the meantime, your only responsibility is to protect yourself and control your own life. It's difficult at times to distinguish between our own experiences and others', but practicing these dream techniques can certainly help.

WHAT ABOUT CHILDREN'S NIGHTMARES AND RECURRING DREAMS?

Dreams that seem very real and are also extremely upsetting may be past-life karma (old lessons unlearned) that needs to be resolved without need for physical experience. Children often have nightmares due to past-life remembrances. The past lives they are experiencing in their dreams may directly relate to the life they are now living.

We can help them by asking questions about their dreams and letting them talk about them or act them out in play. You may offer suggestions as to how they can imagine turning a monster into a friend, even hiring him as a bodyguard! Offer the monster food? Maybe the monster's just hungry. Remind the children that any resources they want or need are available in their dreams.

The most effective solution is to teach your children to sing HU, as introduced previously in this book. Your children will love this sound. Many children still feel so close to the heavenly worlds that they remember this love song to God in some level of their being.

The most effective solution is to teach your children to sing HU.

Also, you can tell your children about the love and protection they have from the Dream Master, the Mahanta, anytime they ask for it. Tell them they can invite the Dream Master to be their friend, protector, or bodyguard in their dreams.

Be creative with your solutions, and also ask your children what their ideas may be. You'll be amazed.

Being childlike in your attitude and imagination will help both your children and you navigate the shoals of life and the obstacles in your dreams.

The other side of dream communication—the positive, loving experiences—can be wonderful in the heavenly worlds of your dreams. The next chapter will take you into the fascinating world of communicating in dreams.

9

Dreams of Communication

At the base level, the physical body dies. People then take up residence on the Astral Plane. It's pretty much the same as here on earth, except they may take on a younger appearance. But the personality itself is extinguished when they go down the slide of reincarnation and come back to earth.

This explains why you see your loved ones or even pets in your dreams after they have passed on.

—Harold Klemp, *The Slow Burning Love of God*, Mahanta Transcripts, Book 13[1]

SOUL TO SOUL IN THE DREAM STATE

Soul is a marvelous, unlimited being. You and I are Soul, and as Soul we have the ability to visit the heavenly worlds in our dreams. Many people have visited loved ones in their dreams, whether alive on this earth or not!

When there's no other way to communicate with someone, dreams can be a wonderful vehicle. Whether the person with whom you want to communicate has passed on from this world or simply gone on a cruise

You and I are Soul, and as Soul we have the ability to visit the heavenly worlds in our dreams.

or is unreachable or out of touch due to a misunderstanding or family feud, you may find this aspect of dreaming to be quite helpful!

Stephanie's grandmother had just passed away. Stephanie was wondering where her grandmother was living, now that she was gone. Her dream showed her:

Stephanie's grandmother was sitting in a rocking chair, in a structure that was somewhat like a house. Her home was on a high mesa in what Stephanie perceived as an alternative reality. Everything seemed a little surreal, and her grandmother's hair was bright orange! So was the hair of some other beings that surrounded her.

Stephanie wondered where this place could be and realized it was a kind of cleansing place, where her grandmother would have time to heal and reflect on her life. The orange-colored hair indicated a place of healing to Stephanie, since orange light is often used in healing.

Stephanie's father died about one year later. She had been grieving and wondering how and where he was. Then she had this dream:

Stephanie was with her mother and sister visiting her father in a beautiful place which reminded her of the East Coast. She saw a lovely white house with a white picket fence. The scene was set against a deep blue sky with puffy white clouds. She watched her dad step out of a brand-new station wagon. Right then, Stephanie sensed a ball of maroon-colored light hanging over her shoulder. She felt very good and

> Stephanie's grandmother had just passed away. Stephanie was wondering where her grandmother was living, now that she was gone.

happy as her father approached and said, "It's so good to be here with all my girls again." A voice from the colored light said to her, "You know your dad is still going to be dead when you wake up."

But Stephanie woke up still feeling good and even happy, because she felt she had, in reality, visited her father and they had communicated Soul to Soul. She knew the voice was warning her so she wouldn't be sad when she woke up. The voice was the Dream Master, whom Stephanie had never met, but nonetheless, he was there to help her through this. Stephanie could ask the Dream Master for help in getting back to that place to visit her dad or have other dream experiences of love anytime she wanted.

A note of interest: some ECK Masters wear maroon-colored robes or clothing. Thus a maroon-colored light could indicate the presence of an ECK Master or the Dream Master as a spiritual guide. The Mahanta, the Dream Master, will often appear as a blue light or blue star.

The Mahanta, the Dream Master, will often appear as a blue light or blue star.

WOULD YOU LIKE TO COMMUNICATE WITH SOMEONE WHO HAS MOVED ON TO THE HEAVENLY WORLDS?

When a family member dies and leaves you with some unfinished thoughts to express, you can use your dreams to communicate those thoughts or feelings.

Having just been informed that her mother was dying, Marianne got on the first flight to Phoenix. Marianne's mother died before she could reach her. Marianne felt so empty and sad inside. She and her mother hadn't always gotten along very well. Marianne wanted to tell her mother how much she'd grown to love and respect her, even if she didn't always agree with her.

In Marianne's last conversation with her mother when her mother was just feeling "a little under the weather," the two women had had yet another argument. This time it was about Marianne's engagement to someone of another religion. Often conversations with her mother would begin in a friendly, yet restrained manner and end in a full-blown argument.

Now Marianne was beside herself with remorse and didn't know what to do. Her sister, Gwen, who studies dreams, said to her, "Why don't you try communicating with Mom in your dreams. After all, she hasn't died, only her body has!"

"Well, I've got no alternative, have I?" said Marianne. She followed Gwen's advice. The following is the technique she used, if you would like to try it.

Get out your journal, and write a letter to your loved one or whomever you are trying to complete communication with, just as if the other person were still alive (they are, as Soul!).

Dream Technique: Soul to Soul

1. Get out your journal, and write a letter to your loved one or whomever you are trying to complete communication with, just as if the other person were still alive (they are, as Soul!). Say everything in the letter that you've been wanting to say to them. Counselors recommend writing letters to deceased loved ones to help people through the grieving process.[2]

2. Search yourself to be sure you've said every-thing you're feeling and thinking. Write the words in the way that feels right to you.

3. In whatever way you pray, ask God to take this letter and deliver it. Free your heart of any burden, knowing it has been done. Go to sleep.

4. Whenever you awaken, even if it's in the middle of the night, jot down any images, thoughts, or feelings that come to mind, whether from your dreams or not. Look at them later to see the possible meaning in them. Perhaps it will be clear, perhaps it will take a while to sort out. More images or experiences may come later. Repeat this exercise anytime you wish.

In whatever way you pray, ask God to take this letter and deliver it. Free your heart of any burden, knowing it has been done. Go to sleep.

THE SAME TECHNIQUE CAN BE USED FOR EVERYDAY COMMUNICATION PROBLEMS

When a situation has you tied up in knots, you can untie those knots very gently by communicating with your friend, coworker, or family member in the dream state. Donna did just that.

Donna's boss was becoming more and more dif-ficult for her to understand. He simply couldn't be reasoned with in matters of marketing trends for this year! He seemed to be stuck in old patterns that worked well in the past. Sales were heading downhill fast. His solution was to do more of what used to work instead of risk trying something new.

All of Donna's marketing experience told her that doing something different and unique was almost always the key to success. Donna was frustrated beyond her ability to keep her mouth shut much longer. However, if she opened it, would it cost her this job?

Luckily, Donna knew about the "Soul to Soul" dream technique, and decided to try it. Donna first asked inwardly for her boss's permission to talk with him in the dream state. Calling on all her powers of imagination, Donna then visualized herself talking with her boss in the dream state. She also visualized a happy ending, whatever it might be. Donna knew she could not and should not try to control another person, but she could control herself and her own life, and she would do so now by imagining a pleasant outcome, surrendering everything to God for the best results.

Donna also picked up her journal and wrote a letter to her boss that she would never send, as in the dream technique. Then she went to sleep with a more peaceful heart than she'd had in months. Here's what she dreamed:

Donna's boss walked into her office and said to her, "Donna, we've tried everything we know, and it hasn't worked. What would you suggest we do now? I'm open to any suggestions you have. At this point, we have nothing to lose."

Donna looked up at her boss and smiled very slowly, as if she was thinking of a grand plan that had just come to her. She said to her boss, "Let's look at a new idea that will use some of your expertise in the area of hot-air balloons!" Donna watched as the look of dejection and failure on her boss's face turned to one of excitement and youthful enthusiasm.

> Donna then visualized herself talking with her boss in the dream state. She also visualized a happy ending, whatever it might be.

Waking up with a smile, Donna realized that in her waking life she had missed one very important point when trying to convince her boss of anything. She hadn't thought of a way to utilize his skills. He was getting older, feeling outdated and worn out. She needed to help him rekindle his enthusiasm! That day, she decided firmly, she would talk with him at the first opening.

Later that day, just as in her dream, her boss did walk into her office and said, "Donna, we need to do something. What do you suggest?" Donna was so excited that her enthusiasm carried over to her boss, and he did indeed look and act younger! The idea worked, and the company moved forward.

Alex tried the same dream communication technique for a relationship problem. He felt that his relationship with his wife, Beth, was surely coming to an end, and he couldn't bear it. They had gotten along so well when they were first married. What had happened?

It seemed now every time they tried to talk with each other, one or the other stormed away, not willing to listen. They were both at fault, and he knew it. But how could he stop this downward spiral? Alex decided to try communicating with her in the dream state, as a friend had suggested. Here's the dream he had after following the "Soul to Soul" technique:

Beth was sitting on the couch reading the newspaper when Alex walked in. She looked up, and her face had a look of fear on it, as though he were going to hurt her in some way. He saw right through the newspaper to Beth's heart. It was glowing with light

> Later that day, just as in her dream, her boss did walk into her office and said, "Donna, we need to do something. What do you suggest?"

and love, but it had a small crack in it. Alex realized how much she loved him, but she had been so hurt by their arguments that her heart was breaking. He went over to her and simply held her for a very long time. She looked up at him with tears in her eyes and said, "This was all I really wanted. Just to know that you still love me and care about me. Sometimes I just need to be held, but I'm afraid to ask when I see how busy and frustrated and tired you are these days."

Alex woke up knowing just what to do. Beth was right there for him to hold, so he did. Then he let her know she was loved very much. Swallowing his pride, he apologized to her for all the times he had walked away in anger.

The positive response he got was well worth any ego deflation he had to endure! Beth even apologized to Alex, letting him know she appreciated his perception of her needs.

When a situation is hard to handle because of the emotional energy and force it has, dream communication may be a solution.

Alex was excited about using the dream state to continue working out difficult communication problems in the future.

SOMEONE MAY BE TRYING TO COMMUNICATE WITH YOU IN DREAMS

When a situation is hard to handle because of the emotional energy and force it has, dream communication may be a solution. However, the person communicating with you in your dreams may be unaware they are doing so. This happened to me when my mother was very ill and close to death.

My mother had been diagnosed with cancer one year before, and she had done very well for her age with surgery and chemotherapy. Her attitude was always positive, so I had hoped that she would live for many more years. Although she had already lived longer than most people, I couldn't seem to accept that she might leave so soon. She and I had just become friends a few years before, after nearly thirty-five years of feeling distant.

My mother must have somehow known I didn't want to accept her death. I had several dreams with her like this one:

I was getting ready for a party with some friends of different ages. My mother was evidently invited too, for she walked into the room wearing a long black dress, looking young and lovely. I complimented her on how she looked. She just smiled and said, "I'm not going to be around here much longer, you know."

When I awoke from the dream, I felt at peace about her body's death. She would be moving on to a place where she'd be younger and stronger. The dream even helped me to help her later when she was getting ready to let go. I told her about the dream, and she laughed, delighted that she might look so great in the heavenly worlds!

ANIMALS MAY TELL YOU
WHAT THEY NEED IN YOUR DREAMS

Cathy's horse King was not happy. She could tell by the way he held back when Cathy wanted to mount him, even bareback. At feeding time he ate his hay, but none of his other grain mix. Cathy called the vet.

After asking Cathy all kinds of questions, the vet left the barn saying, "I wish I could tell you

My mother must have somehow known I didn't want to accept her death. I had several dreams with her.

something, Cathy, but I can't. The only thing I can say is we'll have to wait until more symptoms appear. In the meantime, try to think of what might be upsetting him."

Cathy was used to working with her dreams, so she thought, *Why don't I ask King what's bothering him in my dreams tonight?*

Cathy did the "Soul to Soul" technique, and here's what she dreamed:

King was running and playing in a large open area by the river, right on Cathy's property. He rolled in the mud having himself a good old time.

Cathy instantly knew the meaning of this dream. She definitely believed that animals were Soul, too, and that they knew more than people gave them credit for. Cathy had been meaning to fence in that area for the horses for a whole year at least, and those rascals knew it! Now King, the one who loved to run the most, was starting a rebellion and the other horses would probably soon follow. What was a woman to do but listen to her horse?

The minute Cathy started work on that fence, King's appetite improved and he willingly let Cathy ride him, saddled or not! She learned to listen to her dreams, especially when she needed to help her animal friends.

Many people communicate in their dreams when there's no other way, especially when they're in love.

WHEN SOMEONE IS FAR AWAY, DREAMS CAN BRING YOU CLOSER

Many people communicate in their dreams when there's no other way, especially when they're in love.

The dream state can also be used to communicate when time is short in waking life.

When my husband and I first decided we would get married we lived on nearly opposite ends of the country. The phone bills got pretty high, so we decided to communicate as much as we could in the dream state. The phone bills didn't get any lower, but we sure got a lot of "busy work" settled. Sometimes we were working together, sometimes we were planning our wedding, and sometimes we were putting our house in order.

It was amazing at how easy all of this was when we were finally in our home together and married. The wedding and honeymoon were like they were planned in heaven, the move-in went smoothly, and we found places for everything in our one-bedroom apartment. Also, we were able to work together in a small space for ten months—something that would have driven most people really crazy, and only drove us a little crazy!

A loving dream communication was shared by another couple who had to spend their first Christmas apart. Yvonne was staying at a cabin in the mountains, and Jeremy needed to stay at home to work. Before parting they said to each other, "See you in the dream state."

The first night apart, Yvonne could feel Jeremy's presence in the dream state. He was with her, hugging her. Yvonne could feel the reality of his love and warmth.

The next morning, she couldn't wait to call him. When she finally did, she discovered that he'd had the exact same experience!

The first night apart, Yvonne could feel Jeremy's presence in the dream state. He was with her, hugging her.

WANT TO WORK WITH SOMEONE IN YOUR DREAMS?

To communicate consciously with someone in your dreams, you can ask someone if they are willing to work with you on this. It could be someone with whom you are starting a business or leading a seminar. It may be a family member with whom you would like to work out some differences of opinion. Perhaps a church associate and you would like to plan a fundraiser, but you're not quite sure how to work together yet or what should be done.

There are limitless uses for the dream state. Why not use more of the time we have instead of just sleeping and being unaware? Incredible spiritual adventures await us in our dreams.

Incredible spiritual adventures await us in our dreams.

10

Spiritual Experiences
through Dreams

*Begin remembering your dreams to get an
idea of who and what you are as Soul.*

*You'll see things; you'll gain wisdom. Some-
times you go to Temples of Golden Wisdom.
Sometimes an ECK Master will be teaching
you in the dream state, giving you spiritual
exercises. These exercises can help you travel
further into the dream worlds or get deeper
insights into the secret laws of life.*

—Harold Klemp, *The Slow Burning Love of God,*
Mahanta Transcripts, Book 14[1]

Begin remem-
bering your
dreams to get
an idea of who
and what you
are as Soul.

reams have fascinated, assisted, and uplifted
spiritual seekers through the ages, as exem-
plified by the following quote from, "Why Study
Dreams? A Religious Studies Perspective," an article
by Doniger and Bulkley, published in *Dreaming,* Journal of the Association for the Study of Dreams. "Religion was the original field of dream study. The earliest

writings we have on dreams are primarily texts on their religious and spiritual significance. . . . Dreams are important religious phenomena in virtually all the world's religious traditions."[2]

The article also states that many religions throughout history viewed dreams as messages sent by gods or spirits. The Talmud, an ancient collection of Jewish teachings, has sophisticated discourse on dream interpretation. Dreams are described in detail in the Upanishads, seventh-century Hindu texts. Synesios, a Christian bishop of Ptolemais in the fifth century A.D., wrote a treatise, *On Dreams*.

From the same article: "Dreams are, and always have been, a powerful source of religious experience and insight. Phenomenologically speaking, it is a plain fact that dreams do at times speak directly and powerfully to people's basic spiritual concerns. Many modern dream researchers have, to their credit, recognized this fact. But . . . have not always had the conceptual resources needed to examine adequately the spiritual dimensions of dreams. Here is where religious studies must be brought into the dialogue, for religious studies can provide the vocabularies, methods, and models we need to understand fully this important aspect of human dream experience."

Many religions today have lost their dream teachings or have forgotten their importance. In Eckankar, dreams are respected as a means for Soul to express Itself and listen to God. Dreams can also be a way to have tremendous spiritual experiences and experience powerful doses of divine love.

> Many religions today have lost their dream teachings or have forgotten their importance. In Eckankar, dreams are respected as a means for Soul to express Itself and listen to God.

Conscious Spiritual Experiences Often Begin in the Dream State

In her dream Myra walked toward a beautiful stained-glass window with a six-pointed blue star in its center. The star began to glow, faintly increasing in intensity. Myra felt like the light would reach out and touch her with its brilliance. She felt an overpowering wave of love, the likes of which she'd never experienced in her life.

Myra woke from the dream feeling very happy, but she had no idea what it meant. Years later she visited the Temple of ECK, the home of her new religion, Eckankar. When she looked up at the ceiling in the sanctuary, Myra saw the very same blue star she had seen in her dream. It was even made of stained glass! Tears of joy and understanding came to her eyes. Myra felt more blessed than ever before. Her dream had been a real spiritual experience!

Anyone can have spiritual experiences in their dreams. Some people are aware they have had a special dream, like Myra, and not know what it means until later in life. Something may strike a chord of recognition, such as the blue star did for Myra.

Anyone can have spiritual experiences in their dreams.

Some people have the gift to be aware that they've had a spiritual dream, like Tony.

Tony had always wanted to know what God was like. He had a historical and biblical knowledge of God from his upbringing, but to experience directly what God was like—why that would be incredible! This desire haunted him until he almost felt desperate. Why shouldn't he be able to experience some aspect of God directly? Church was always uplifting and joyful in some way, but Tony still didn't feel any closer to God since he didn't really know what God was like as a being.

A friend had talked with Tony about ways to become more aware of spiritual experiences in dreams. Tony decided to use a dream technique. After all, what did he have to lose? It took ten days of trying the technique, but Tony was determined to have his experience. This was what happened in his dream on the tenth night:

Running along a river, Tony was feeling light and free as he always did when he ran. The air was sweet, with a light breeze. The sun was soft and warm, and the sound of the river soothed him. Because he felt so light, he felt like he could keep running forever, or even fly! Just as he had that thought, he began to rise off the ground and fly directly toward the sun!

Amazing as it seemed, Tony had absolutely no fear. He somehow knew that it would be OK. The closer he got to the sun, the brighter it got. However, it did not become hot, as he expected. It simply began to surround him with a feeling of belonging, as if he was a part of this magnificent scene and not just an observer. There were no words, but Tony felt as though he was being told that he was loved greatly and always would be, no matter how imperfect he thought he was.

Tony was thrilled when he awoke. He quickly wrote down his dream, and at the end of it he wrote, "Now I know that you don't have to have a near-death experience to experience God! What a blessing. Thank you!"

He wrote, "Now I know that you don't have to have a near-death experience to experience God! What a blessing. Thank you!"

Perhaps Tony's story will remind you that you've had uplifting feelings or spiritual experiences in your own dreams.

SOME SPIRITUAL DREAMS WILL BRING YOU MORE FREEDOM

Carolyn was new to the teachings of Eckankar. She was learning so much, as well as finding great joy in her life. Carolyn was open to her dream experiences and the lessons she could learn from them.

One dream Carolyn had took place at the Temple of ECK, the spiritual center for Eckankar in Chanhassen, Minnesota. The Temple is surrounded by lovely paths called contemplation trails. Carolyn describes her dream this way:

I was walking along the contemplation trails having a wonderful time. Suddenly I came upon a wall that stretched as far as I could see. As I looked both ways, I instantly turned into a bulldozer. As soon as the tip of the bulldozer blade touched the wall, the wall shattered like an eggshell. Then I went on my way.

Carolyn said this dream meant to her that "roadblocks are an illusion, and I have the power to move through them."

WOULD YOU LIKE TO HAVE A CONSCIOUS SPIRITUAL EXPERIENCE IN YOUR DREAMS?

One of the spiritual experiences people can have in their dreams is Soul Travel. This means simply that, as Soul, you can visit the heavenly worlds—

One of the spiritual experiences people can have in their dreams is Soul Travel.

your inner worlds—by leaving your body during sleep or by consciously shifting your attention to the heavenly worlds and having an experience there.

Most people already do this while dreaming. Some have had conscious out-of-body experiences while on an operating table, like the story in chapter 4. Others have had near-death experiences. You don't have to go to such extremes if you study the teachings of Eckankar and learn to Soul Travel beyond your day-to-day existence. And you can enhance your own religious beliefs and experiences by doing so.

Eckankar books have great spiritual exercises, including Soul Travel techniques and dream exercises with a spiritual focus. I would recommend the book *The Spiritual Exercises of ECK,* by Harold Klemp, for more spiritual dream exercises. Here's a dream technique from that book. It can help you Soul Travel in your dreams![3]

Hu is a special word, the ancient name for God.

Dream Technique: Dreams, Soul Travel, and Love

Just before you go to sleep, sit quietly on your bed. Close your eyes. Chant HU very softly, or if someone is in the room with you, chant it silently to yourself. HU is a special word, the ancient name for God. You could call it the manifested Word or the Sound; it has a power of its own.

As you take the time to sit there and chant HU, the name of God, you are making a commitment with Divine Spirit. Chant HU in a long, drawn-out way for three or four or five minutes, and let yourself settle down. Then wait for a few more minutes before starting the next step.

For those who have been unable to remember their dreams, simply chant the word *dream* spelled out. Chant it out loud, letter by letter: D-R-E-A-M. Do this for about five minutes. Next chant the same thing quietly for a few minutes, and then just go to sleep. As you are falling asleep, say, "I would like to remember a significant spiritual dream." With this method, you are asking for truth to come through the dream state.

Some of you want Soul Travel, which is usually an advanced state beyond the dream state. Again, sit on your bed or on the floor, shut your eyes, and look into your Spiritual Eye. This is located at a point just above and between the eyebrows. Don't expect to see anything there; just chant HU, the holy name of God.

Then spell out *Soul Travel*, chanting each separate letter: S-O-U-L T-R-A-V-E-L. Do this about three times out loud and then three times quietly.

Those who have Soul Traveled may now want to go to the higher state of direct knowingness, without having to go through the intermediary stages. Dreams and Soul Travel

As you are falling asleep, say, "I would like to remember a significant spiritual dream."

are helpful and important, but at some point you outgrow them.

Simply chant the words *divine love.* Originally I was going to give it as L-O-V-E, but some people would mix it up with human love. The word *divine* takes it beyond human love. Divine love brings you all forms of love, including human love. To limit it to the usual definition of love is like working from the bottom, instead of working from the top of spirituality.

So, chant D-I-V-I-N-E L-O-V-E. This means you seek the highest form of love, which brings all blessings to you.

—Harold Klemp,
The Spiritual Exercises of ECK

Keep an eye out for those dreams that have commonplace scenes but are filled with love.

SOME SPIRITUAL DREAMS MAY SEEM COMMONPLACE

Keep an eye out for those dreams that have commonplace scenes but are filled with love. After all, the greatest of God's attributes is love. Often the heavenly worlds appear as earth does, with scenes we can relate to.

Glenn had a dream with that subtle commonplace feeling in it. In the dream:

Glenn was riding his bicycle down a broad avenue, looking for Love Street. The surroundings felt very familiar, so he knew he was close, but he couldn't seem to find the street. In his peripheral vision Glenn spotted a slim, dark-haired man in a blue suit who was wearing glasses. The man was waving at him and smiling happily.

Glenn made a U-turn to see who was waving. Perhaps it was an old forgotten friend. It seemed there was some kind of bond between them, but Glenn could not remember what kind of connection they had. Glenn stopped in front of the man, who was still smiling at Glenn as if he had indeed found a long-lost friend. The thing Glenn noticed most about the man, besides the kindness in his heart, was his penetrating gaze.

Glenn woke up feeling happy and carefree. When he went into work that day, he found a pink slip in his mailbox. *Oh no,* he thought, *I've been laid off! Why was I feeling so good this morning? Doesn't this just beat it all!* But somehow, Glenn still felt the love.

A few years and a few more rough experiences later, Glenn found himself looking at a picture of a man who looked very familiar. It was the man in his dream! The photo was on a poster announcing an Eckankar seminar in town. The man, Harold Klemp, was said to be the spiritual leader of this religion. Glenn simply could not miss the opportunity to meet someone from his dreams. How awesome!

When Glenn actually saw the man speaking, he realized it was the same man from his dream and the love was still there. Glenn also figured out that this love had never really left him, because every time he went through big changes in his life, such as when he lost his job, it was there. The love was a subtle presence that he could never seem to describe to himself or anyone else.

> The thing Glenn noticed most about the man, besides the kindness in his heart, was his penetrating gaze.

Glenn also became very clear about the fact that he and this spiritual leader were indeed old friends. He also knew that the man was not just a man, but something like a guardian angel, helping him here on earth as well as in his dreams and in the heavenly worlds. Thanks to his dream, Glenn knew that his spiritual teacher, the Mahanta, would always be with him.

While exploring the spiritual aspects of dreaming, don't be surprised if you meet someone here on earth who is just like your dream guide or guardian angel! They will often take physical form to work more closely with us in a way we can comprehend. Here's an example.

Justine was always telling her mother about different dreams she had with a playmate she called Rubber Tires. Her mother would just laugh and go on with her work, wondering where this child of hers could come up with such a funny name for a dream playmate.

As the child grew, she forgot about Rubber Tires, until one day when she was visiting the church a friend of hers attended. It was the Temple of ECK, which had pictures of several Masters who helped in God's work. Justine took a closer look at a portrait of one of these Masters. Her mouth dropped open as she realized who he was. She squeaked out the words, "I know this man. He used to be in my dreams all the time!"

The friend said, "His name is Rebazar Tarzs."

"That even sounds like what I used to call him, Rubber Tires!" Justine said. She knew then and

> While exploring the spiritual aspects of dreaming, don't be surprised if you meet someone here on earth who is just like your dream guide or guardian angel!

there that dreams are real experiences and that she had always been loved and protected.

Becoming aware of ourselves spiritually helps us accept the spiritual experiences in our dreams, as Justine was able to do.

LUCID DREAMING CAN MAKE YOU MORE AWARE OF YOUR SPIRITUAL SELF

Being awake and aware in your dreams is called "lucid dreaming" by dream experts like Stephen LaBerge, author and researcher who did original research on lucid dreams.[4]

Lucid dreaming simply means that you're observing and experiencing the dream in full consciousness as Soul, even though the body is asleep. While your body is asleep, Soul is awake to greater states of awareness. You don't need to have lucid dreams for this to happen, because it's happening all the time regardless. However, lucid dreaming is a way to gain more awareness and control in your dreams, and therefore in your day-to-day life. After all, life is just another kind of dream, when you look at it from the viewpoint of Soul, awake and aware.

> While your body is asleep, Soul is awake to greater states of awareness.

Five to ten percent of the population has lucid dreams.[5] Jayne Gackenbach, an experimental psychologist at the University of Northern Iowa, found that lucid dreamers are less likely to be depressed or neurotic than the general population.[6] What a great side benefit! She also discovered that people who do not have the ability to have lucid dreams can develop it, if they are motivated and have good dream recall.

Dream Technique: Heaven's Waiting

1. Write in your dream journal something like this: I would like to have a spiritual experience in my dream that is of God's will.

2. Add anything specific you may want to experience, such as God's love, God's wisdom, or the Light and Sound of God. Write it down, and after it write something like, "Thy will be done" to release it to the will of Divine Spirit. Letting go is the quickest way to have the experiences you want.

3. Go to sleep saying or singing a prayer, holy word, phrase you may know, or a love song to God, such as HU, which was described in the earlier exercise.

   As you drift off to sleep, see yourself in the most beautiful place you can imagine. It could be an idyllic scene in nature or a magnificent Temple of Golden Wisdom.

4. Write down absolutely anything that you experience in your dream, no matter how commonplace it may seem. Spiritual experiences are not always dramatic or bold but sometimes soft and subtle as a butterfly kiss.

As you drift off to sleep, see yourself in the most beautiful place you can imagine.

I find that, for me, the best way to have a lucid dream is to ask for it right before I fall asleep. During the period of time before sleep comes, you may begin to see unusual images and perhaps feel as though you are weightless. That time period is called the hypnogogic state by dream experts. Some connect these sensations and visions to certain types of spiritual and out-of-body experiences.

It may take many days or weeks to have a lucid dream, but I know I must be persistent. Then I try to stay as aware as possible while falling asleep. I watch every detail on the screen of my mind until I find myself in a different environment than in my bed at home. An example of a lucid dream I had was this:

I was lying on the ground in a sunny, spacious place. I became aware that I was dreaming. It seemed like a golden kind of place, with a soft kind of wheat to lie on. I was relaxed but grew wary as I saw some people coming toward me. They began to become hostile, so I simply got up and flew away!

I felt so free when I woke up that day. Freedom was what I really needed to cultivate. What fun it was to be able to fly on my own volition! You can too! Try this in any dream you wish. Soul can do anything, go anywhere, and be anything It wants to be. Would you like to experience being a cat or an eagle? How about a dream experience of something you have always wanted to do for a living? You can experience it in your dreams while fully aware and see if it really is for you.

Perhaps there is a challenge in your life or a habit you are trying to overcome but haven't had much success with. Lucid dreaming can be a way to practice in your dreams so your waking-life challenge is made easier. Fred had such a challenge.

Lucid dreaming can be a way to practice in your dreams so your waking-life challenge is made easier.

Fred decided he wanted to eat more slowly. He'd been wolfing down his food for years, paying the price with indigestion. *If lucid dreaming works for controlling your life, why not try it for this,* he thought.

Following Stephen LaBerge's research on lucid dreaming, Fred told himself every night he would have a lucid dream. Finally he did. Here was his lucid dream:

Fred told himself every night he would have a lucid dream. Finally he did.

An orange balloon was sailing past Fred as he sat on someone's front porch. He was not sure whose house he was visiting but decided to wait until someone came out. Since he was aware in his dream, he decided to create a barbecue right there on the porch, with a lot of his favorite food—barbecued chicken, corn on the cob, and fresh spinach salad with blue-cheese dressing. He could hardly wait to sink his teeth into it. His mouth was already watering.

Then Fred remembered his goal for the dream and decided to take control right then and there. He made himself enjoy the aroma of the food, taking it in with a deep breath, slowly helping himself to whatever he wanted. Sitting down to his feast, Fred vowed to chew every bite until it was almost liquid. This seemed like the longest dream he had ever had, but he kept his promise.

When Fred woke up, he felt different somehow, but he couldn't quite put his finger on it. He got up to eat breakfast, remembering his lucid dream of the night before and being proud of himself for having met his goal. Could he do the same thing now? Somehow, he knew he could. It would take discipline and perhaps more work in the dream state, but now he knew he had the self-discipline he'd wanted for so long.

Other areas of Fred's life changed too. He was able to discipline himself more at work and in his exercise program. He felt more in control of his life than ever before.

FREE YOURSELF IN YOUR DREAMS

Would you like to be able to have lucid dreams? Try the following exercise, and be diligent. It may take quite a few days or even weeks to have a lucid dream.

Dream Technique: Lucid Dreaming

1. Just before falling asleep, tell yourself you will wake up in your dream, and that you will be aware and in control of everything. Watch yourself falling asleep for as long as you can. You may even find yourself almost immediately in another world, in some inner experience.

2. When you do wake up in your dream, control it as if you were directing a movie. You can tell the actors what to do simply by using your creative imagination. No words are needed. You simply make things happen from inside you.

3. Write down anything you remember upon awakening.

Watch yourself falling asleep for as long as you can. You may even find yourself almost immediately in another world, in some inner experience.

Here's another lucid dreaming technique, from *The Spiritual Exercises of ECK* by Harold Klemp.

Dream Technique: Watching Yourself Fall Asleep

Every night before retiring, relax on the bed. Watch the process of going to sleep. Keep your attention on the point between the eyebrows, the Spiritual Eye.

As your body relaxes and your mind settles down, that change in viewpoint takes place which we call sleep. Maintain the attitude of awareness. You will note your body getting quiet and your thoughts settling down. Hearing is often the last to leave the human consciousness. You will be detached on the borderline state, as though in a dream.

Then you will come into another state of beingness. This is characterized by a clarity of mental vision. It is not an unconscious state like a mental fog, but a level of awareness beyond the limits of normal human expression.

This viewpoint may last a moment or for several hours. With practice it may last through the whole night.

To hold on to this lucidity, you need to maintain a delicate balance between not becoming too emotional and not forgetting that you are dreaming.

Then you will come into another state of beingness. This is characterized by a clarity of mental vision.

What has happened? As the body rests, you awaken in the . . . Soul body. You find yourself in eternity, overcoming death. This is the freedom which is spoken about so often in Eckankar.

Spiritual experiences can go beyond dreaming, yet still happen in a dreamlike state. The next chapter will help you identify different types of spiritual and dreamlike experiences you may have had in daily life.

Spiritual experiences can go beyond dreaming.

11

Worlds beyond the Dream World

The waking state right here is very much alive compared to the dream you had last night. But those who have had a Soul Travel experience realize that the Soul Travel experience is that much more dynamic than just being aware here in the physical waking state.

Some of you know this. You've had a Soul Travel experience of one kind of another—where it is so clear, and you have such insight and perception of divine love that you cannot imagine it in your normal human state.

—Harold Klemp, *The Secret of Love*, Mahanta Transcripts, Book 14[1]

Shortly after I got married, my mother-in-law told me of a very interesting experience she'd had while fully awake. She was experiencing a lot of pain following a car accident. To overcome the pain, she would think about the family's property in Hawaii and how wonderful it would be to visit it right then. Suddenly she was there, smelling the

> To overcome the pain, she would think about the family's property in Hawaii and how wonderful it would be to visit it right then. Suddenly she was there.

sweet fragrance of plumeria blossoms and watching the wind in the fields of sugarcane on their property. The sun was warm and comforting.

Later, she asked her doctor about the experience. She said, "Is it true, doctor, that when you're in so much pain, you can go somewhere else and feel the breezes and smell the flowers?" He said, "Yes, that's called an out-of-body experience and some people have those. Not everyone has them, but you did."

DREAMLIKE EXPERIENCES BEYOND THIS WORLD CAN EASILY HAPPEN WHILE AWAKE

Have you ever been driving and found yourself suddenly back in the car? Where had you been? Perhaps you were thinking of what type of pizza you would order at the pizza shop once you got there. The aroma of freshly baked pizza and the bright, checkered tablecloths drew you there in your thoughts. When you realized you almost missed your turn, you came back to your body.

Just writing the above paragraph makes me want to go to that pizza shop. Because I'm imagining it, and imagination is one of the most powerful tools we possess. It's our divine gift, as Soul. Think about it for a moment.

Every action you take is preceded by a thought. Thoughts are images shot with feeling, color, sounds, smells, and tastes. If you think about going to the movies, images of the bright screen in a dark theater filled with the aroma of freshly popped popcorn are enough to get you off the couch and moving.

Although going to a pizza shop or the movies in

> Every action you take is preceded by a thought. Thoughts are images shot with feeling, color, sounds, smells, and tastes.

your imagination may not seem like a very spiritual experience, it is. It's how we move into the next state of consciousness, or awareness, as Soul. In Eckankar we call it Soul Travel.

Sometimes Soul Travel is as commonplace as imagining yourself doing the grocery shopping and being in the store, while you plan the best route through the store. At other times it's a definite experience of being in another place or time, in a higher world filled with a tremendous, unbelievable amount of love. I had a hint of one such experience recently.

Lying awake a few nights ago, I was thinking about two close friends in different parts of the country. They were both in the middle of difficult moves, and I felt a lot of love and compassion for them. I felt a desire to take them away with me to a fun and playful setting where we could all just enjoy a rest, relaxing in the sun together.

The feeling of being with them both was so strong, I felt like I was really with them. We were surrounded by an inexplicable feeling of pure, unconditional love. The love was so strong, it made me want to get up and call them. However, since it was late, I decided to wait until the next day.

I called one of my friends the next day and told her about my experience. I could almost see her mouth fall open as she said, "So did I! I was with you both, and we were all playing. There was so much love, and I felt so free. I really missed you both and wanted to be with you too."

This was another example of Soul Travel. My

Sometimes Soul Travel is as commonplace as imagining yourself doing the grocery shopping and being in the store, while you plan the best route through the store.

body didn't go anywhere, but I was somewhere else as Soul. Since Soul can go beyond the limitations of time and space, it doesn't need to move in order to be in a different time/space. My friend and I were in the same place at the same time in some other world, a world with so much love it's hard to imagine with our minds or human emotions. Soul can experience this tremendous love, and sometimes we remember.

Often, these experiences are for our spiritual awareness and learning. Past-life experiences can also come to us while we are still awake.

Past-life experiences can also come to us while we are still awake.

DREAMLIKE EXPERIENCES WHILE AWAKE CAN BE QUITE EYE-OPENING

Marcia was getting a massage, feeling wonderfully relaxed but fully awake, when suddenly an image began to form, just like in a dream, and played out in her mind's eye. Here's what happened:

A little boy and girl were playing outside, under a shade tree. The little boy broke away and ran up to a wise-looking Asian man. He seemed like a spiritual master of some kind. The boy said to him, "When my sister is happy, I do not like it. It does not make me happy."

The master said to him, "Go and stand in the sunshine and hold your face up to the sun." The boy did as he was told. The master asked him, "How does that make you feel?" The boy said it made him feel happy. The master said, "That is how you should feel for your sister all the time."

Marcia had a sense that the dreamlike experience was a past-life recall. She felt that perhaps the massage triggered some old forgotten memory of a happy time with her spiritual teacher. She did not remember more of that lifetime, but she knew that was not the purpose of this daydream. It was a message of divine love that she should have for herself as well as others. It was a special spiritual experience.

An instance of a daydream experience from a past life came to Sheila as she was wondering where she had known her new romantic interest before.

Suddenly she saw herself in another life, walking up a magnificent staircase with broad, highly polished wooden railings. Coming down the stairs was her beloved, but she was not to reveal this to anyone. She lowered her eyes as she walked past him, because he was of a lower class and she was not allowed to associate with him or anyone of his class. These were the rules of the time, and they both feared the consequences of breaking them.

When Sheila came back to herself, she suddenly knew why she and her new beau were so desperate to be together, as if they had been forced apart. Now she knew why she felt as she did! Once she got to know him well, it all seemed silly, as he was not at all right for her. However, she came away from that brief relationship with two gifts: healing that lifetime of strict obedience to social law and a greater understanding of herself.

It was a message of divine love that she should have for herself as well as others. It was a special spiritual experience.

Waking Soul Travel Experiences Prepare Us for the Unknown

As my mother lay on her deathbed, fully aware that she was dying, she and I had several conversations about death. I told her I was jealous, because she got to go somewhere she would see such pretty lights and hear such beautiful sounds and be free of her physical body.

She told me she was very happy to be going. She had lived a good life. But who knows what happens when we die? she said. After all, no one has come back to tell us! I told her about Elisabeth Kübler-Ross's research and the growing media coverage of near-death experiences, how more people were having the experience of seeing some kind of light.[2]

One day later that week I walked into my mother's room as she was watching her favorite soap opera on TV. She said to me, "There are such beautiful lights on this program that have never been there before!" The lights she saw were not on the television show, but in her own inner worlds.

I was ecstatic. I knew my mother had seen the Light of God, and It was beckoning her on to a higher state of consciousness. She was beginning to open up to the world beyond death, where Soul is eternal.

Later that night my sister-in-law reported hearing my mother say "Freddie" a few times as she was talking to herself in her sleep. Freddie was my father's name, and he died over twenty-five years ago. My mother never remarried, never finding a love like she had with my father.

I knew my mother had seen the Light of God, and It was beckoning her on to a higher state of consciousness.

My brother and I felt she was beginning the journey into the other worlds. Even though she seemed to be communicating with my father in his heavenly home, she was very lucid and clear in her communication with those of us still on earth, right up until she died the next week.

VISITING LOVED ONES IN INNER WORLDS CAN HAVE A TRUE-TO-LIFE FEEL

While still awake, you can visit loved ones in the inner worlds, just as some people do in their dreams.

Michael had a vivid waking experience with his grandfather. Michael's grandfather had been hospitalized for months; he was in a coma. Michael wanted to visit his grandfather, who was far away, and found himself doing just that one day during work. He felt sure he was having a real experience. This is what happened:

Michael was in his grandfather's hospital room watching his grandfather sit up and get out of bed. This seemed very natural to Michael as he and Grandpa walked to the sliding-glass doors and out into the garden together. They sat in the garden and talked for some time.

Michael shared a secret with his grandfather. He said, "Grandpa, I have a spiritual guide who you can talk to if you want. Whenever you are ready, I can introduce you. He can help you when you get ready to leave us."

His grandfather smiled and nodded. Michael's spiritual teacher, the Mahanta, showed up just then,

> While still awake, you can visit loved ones in the inner worlds, just as some people do in their dreams.

and Michael introduced the two men, leaving them to talk. Michael wandered off into the garden. There was a feeling of great love.

Two days later, Michael's grandfather passed on to the heavenly worlds. Michael's experience was real. It was a Soul Travel experience that allowed him to talk with his grandfather one more time. It also helped him let go of his grandfather and may even have helped his grandfather let go of his body without fear.

SPIRITUAL EXERCISES STRENGTHEN OUR SPIRITUAL MUSCLES

In Eckankar we learn to do spiritual exercises that help open us more to Divine Spirit in our lives and to spiritual adventures like Michael's. The benefits are endless, including richer spiritual experiences in dreams or waking life. If you have done any of the dream techniques in this book, you've already done a spiritual exercise.

Doing spiritual exercises daily helps me stay connected with Holy Spirit.

Doing spiritual exercises daily helps me stay connected with Holy Spirit. This way, I am more closely attuned with my inner guidance. My life runs more smoothly, and I feel a greater sense of purpose. I better understand the rough times as part of a greater plan to help me find my way back to God, as we all are doing.

Would you like to have a loving, spiritual experience like those from this and previous chapters? Try the exercise below for at least thirty days or until something happens. Remember that these spiritual experiences can seem almost commonplace. Look for the feelings of freedom and love.

Spiritual Exercise: Looking for Love

1. Before retiring or anytime you are able to relax, sit down with feet flat on the floor or lie down comfortably.

2. Take a few deep breaths. Let all tension release, while opening your heart to God's love. It helps to think about someone or something you love dearly. Perhaps it's a pet or something you love doing very much.

3. Ask God for a spiritual experience you will recognize as such. You may or may not recognize your experience as being a spiritual one, but it helps to ask.

4. Sing HU, the love song to God described in the first chapter. Sing it with love in your heart. If you prefer, sing another holy word or phrase that is dear to you.

5. Most important: Listen. God speaks to us in sound as well as light, and that is God's love song to us. You may hear a sound like music or any sounds of nature. You may even hear a high electrical buzz. You might see light of any color. Or you may experience a simple joy that has some special meaning just for you. Light and Sound are the two basic elements of creation, the essence or divine love of God manifested. It's the way God communicates with us.

6. In your journal write down any experiences, thoughts, or feelings that come to you so that

God speaks to us in sound as well as light, and that is God's love song to us.

> you may look back later and remember your connection with God.

Many people find their spiritual experiences in exercises like the one just given to be very subtle. They may not be aware they had a spiritual experience, because it seems so natural at the time. Sometimes I think, *Oh, that was just my imagination.* I forget that imagination is a divine gift and that if I can imagine it, it is a real experience for Soul.

These experiences may not be out-of-body experiences, but you may feel a greater sense of love, purpose, or gratitude for the smallest things in life. It may be that your interest turns more to service and giving to others. Life can take some wonderful turns when we work with the spiritual tools we're given.

For more spiritual exercises read *The Spiritual Exercises of ECK* by Harold Klemp. For more about your journey home to God as Soul, read the book *The Journey of Soul,* Mahanta Transcripts, Book 1, also by Harold Klemp.[3]

KNOWING IS A QUALITY OF SOUL AND A SOUL EXPERIENCE

Upon awakening from certain dreams, sometimes we just know things. In daily life, we can skip the dream state and go to direct knowing. The spiritual exercise just given is the kind that hones your "knowing" skills when you can trust yourself enough to hear the truth.

Some instances of knowing are almost overpowering, like when I knew we had to move. I resisted

Sometimes I think, Oh, that was just my imagination. I forget that imagination is a divine gift and that if I can imagine it, it is a real experience for Soul.

it, but in my heart I just knew it was right. There was no explanation for it, no logical reason to move, but my husband and I both just knew. Looking back over the year in our new home, we can see that it turned out to be a move that would change the course of our lives and bring us closer to our goals.

Other examples of "knowing" experiences are more subtle, yet persistent. My husband was considering a special training course for health professionals taught by two different companies. There was not much difference in price, yet one company, on the East Coast, seemed very knowledgeable.

However, we didn't have as good a feeling about that company as a second one, based in Houston. The Houston firm had a better support system for follow-up, and the people were willing to take time with us.

For the next two days, it seemed that every time we turned on the radio or television we heard or saw the word *Houston*. That sign from God helped us know even more.

Other less expensive options became available, so my husband asked for clarity from the ECK, or Holy Spirit.

Then he had a very confusing dream. In the dream:

One company was training him in a small room. He decided to go into a larger room where the other company was located. There was so much paperwork, he couldn't carry it all.

Even though he was not entirely sure what the dream meant, he knew what he was supposed to do.

For the next two days, it seemed that every time we turned on the radio or television we heard or saw the word *Houston.* That sign from God helped us know even more.

Houston was it. It didn't seem to make sense financially because the others were less expensive. But again, he knew it was right. In this case, he got what he paid for. He said they put on the best course he's ever attended, and he learned much more than he thought he would. On top of that, he's had great support from them ever since. Hindsight certainly helps to validate what you really did know!

KNOWINGNESS IS A SPIRITUAL SKILL YOU CAN DEVELOP

Is knowing, or intuition, a skill you'd like to improve upon? Try the following dream exercise for thirty days and watch some interesting events take place.

Ask the Dream Master to help you in finding a special door in your inner worlds, that when opened, reveals the answer.

Dream Exercise: A Knack for Knowing

1. Think of a problem or decision that you are in the midst of, no matter how small or insignificant it may seem. Write it in your dream journal.

2. Ask the Dream Master to help you in finding a special door in your inner worlds, that when opened, reveals the answer.

3. Hold the idea lightly in your mind that you will find the door and open it while you're asleep. Tell yourself that when you awaken you will know the answer to your question, whether or not you remember any dreams.

You can practice a similar technique while awake as well. Just ask! Ask the Mahanta or whomever you believe in to help you.

Sometimes I ask simple questions such as, Is this the street I'm looking for? I often get a resounding yes or no inside my head. However, it's not always a word or sound, but a feeling. The words may come in my own voice, as I say to myself, "This is it." It works for me as long as I stay attuned to Divine Spirit, follow the spiritual laws, and keep my heart open.

It's not always easy trusting ourselves to know what's right or true. I've found that practicing with little things, like asking for the right street as in the previous example, works well. The more I listen and follow, the simpler it is to keep listening and following. Then the bigger answers are easier to get from Holy Spirit, as your inner listening skills develop.

Sometimes the right turn may not be where you've chosen to go, but the new direction will help you avoid trouble ahead. Trusting completely in Spirit, after using all of your common sense, is the best way I know to live a life filled with miracles.

Speaking of miracles, they're occurring around us daily, if we only pay attention. Studying waking dreams, the topic of the next chapter, will help you notice these marvelous postcards from God.

Trusting completely in Spirit, after using all of your common sense, is the best way I know to live a life filled with miracles.

12

Life Is But a Dream

Through my study what I have found is that all life is a dream. The dream of everyday living is no more or less a dream than what happens at night during the sleep state. A dream is a dream, but it is also reality, as real as everyday life out here.

Once you get into dreaming and move along further, you begin to realize this.

We begin dream study in ECK with the waking dream. In other words, we look at the ways Divine Spirit is trying to give us hints in everyday life to make things work out better for us.

—Harold Klemp, *How the Inner Master Works*, Mahanta Transcripts, Book 12[1]

Row, Row, Row Your Boat

You may remember the song from grade school usually sung as a round:

Row, row, row your boat gently down the stream;
Merrily, merrily, merrily, merrily,
Life is but a dream.[2]

As in the nursery rhyme above, we're dreaming as much in life as we are in dreams. Life is but a dream. Soul experiences dreams the same way It experiences life and vice versa. That's why it is so nice that we're in a state of temporary physical immobilization when we dream, so we don't act out what we are dreaming about.[3] If we weren't temporarily immobilized, we could potentially harm ourselves or others while dreaming actively. That's how real dreaming is to Soul.

There's actually no difference to Soul between waking life and dream life. Life can even be viewed as a lucid dream that you may be able to control from the viewpoint of Soul.

Because life is so very much like a dream, we can often interpret life experiences just as we interpret our dreams. Sometimes these experiences can come through the Golden-tongued Wisdom.

Golden-tongued Wisdom is a term coined by Harold Klemp. It is divine guidance that usually comes in the form of words, whether written or spoken, that give you insight into your life.

Another form of Golden-tongued Wisdom is the waking dream. This term is used a lot in the Eckankar books and teachings. Waking-dream symbols can be anything which helps you find direction in your life, move forward spiritually, make decisions, and more. These waking dreams may come as visual symbols or words which ring true for you. They confirm that you're heading in the right direction.

For example, a hawk flying nearby might symbolize freedom for you; a fire truck may mean things

> Life can even be viewed as a lucid dream that you may be able to control from the viewpoint of Soul.

are heating up. To someone else, a hawk may be telling her to look higher and a fire truck may mean danger ahead.

These postcards from God are called waking dreams. Interpreting waking dreams is fun to do and brings a lot of insight. Interpreting life as I would a dream has often helped me make decisions when I was completely frustrated. When opposing forces pulled me in different directions, I needed steadfast guidance that could come only from God.

Here's a dramatic example of a waking dream with some Golden-tongued Wisdom in it:

Teresa was in a mild depression. By nature she's a cheerful person. Sadness and despair were quite unusual for her. She knew from her connection with Holy Spirit that she was working through painful old patterns from lifetimes past.

What could she do? Teresa had done everything common sense told her—from eating and sleeping well, to exercise, to filling herself with the Light and Sound of God as much as she knew how. She realized there was something she was missing! She had been to doctors, so Teresa knew she was healthy physically. She also tried some counseling, and it helped for a short time, but then she became depressed again.

Teresa wondered if perhaps she needed help of a different kind. She asked her inner spiritual guide, the Mahanta, "Do I need more therapy?" Then she turned on the television. At that very moment:

An old lady on a comedy show said, "Therapy is good!"

> These post-
> cards from God
> are called
> waking dreams.

Could her answer have been more clear? Teresa felt the old woman represented wisdom. She knew what she had to do, but who should she go to for counseling?

Very shortly thereafter, Teresa was invited to a gathering of health professionals for a birthday party. She met a counselor there she liked instantly. Neither of them had really wanted to go to that party, but something had strongly drawn them both. Once they exchanged phone numbers, they left, knowing they had fulfilled their purpose there.

Teresa did get therapy from this counselor, and her life improved.

By following her guidance through the words on the TV show, and the waking-dream symbol of the old woman which meant wisdom to her, Teresa was able to break through a cycle of hopelessness and have a happier life.

Jennifer also had a waking dream with some important spoken wisdom in it for her.

Challenged by some issues at work, Jennifer was glad her hectic week was over! She was grateful to relax under a shade tree in a park. The day was perfect, the soft sunlight lulled her to sleep, even though her mind still wandered back to her feelings about the issues at work. Right about the time she began to drift off, she heard voices. They became louder until they woke her completely, so she could clearly hear the Golden-tongued Wisdom that was about to come.

A young girl was climbing one of the trees, calling to her family:

> By following her guidance, Teresa was able to break through a cycle of hopelessness and have a happier life.

"Mom, look at me! I don't need Dad anymore!"

The girl was telling her mother that she could climb the tree without any help from her father. However, to Jennifer the words meant something quite different. She knew she was letting go of a certain kind of support and moving to a whole new level in her life. Jennifer was now an adult ready to take on life by herself, ready to be self-supporting, free, and independent. How wonderful it was! She suddenly felt in control of her life, and the concern about issues at work slipped away. The freedom and independence of Soul was shining through.

The words or images we notice most vividly, as Jennifer did, are often those that are trying to speak to us. God's voice, the Holy Spirit, speaks to us in many ways, and waking dreams are a wonderfully fun, sometimes puzzling, always exciting miracle of life. I love the challenge they bring, because it's like deciphering a puzzle about life.

Life gives us messages constantly. We need only look and listen with care.

YOU CAN EVEN ASK FOR YOUR OWN WAKING-DREAM SYMBOLS

Sandra wanted so much to use music as a vehicle for healing. There was a new program she'd heard about. They taught people to play the harp in hospices, and she wanted to be a part of it very badly. Sandra had begun her training in another state, but she was now living in a state where the training was unavailable, or so she thought.

God's voice, the Holy Spirit, speaks to us in many ways, and waking dreams are a wonderfully fun, sometimes puzzling, always exciting miracle of life.

Sandra found a part-time job teaching dance and began working in an office. She was busy and happy with her work, but not completely fulfilled. Something was missing. It was her mission. She needed to be working with the hospice program. One day, out of the blue, a friend living about three hours away called and said, "I'm going to this special training for music and healing in hospices. Why don't you come up here and stay with me and attend the course?" It was the very same course Sandra had been looking for!

Sandra was thrilled. The only thing was, could she afford it? Could she take the time off work and away from her family? Was it really the right thing for her to do after all? After talking this over with her family and getting their OK, Sandra decided to ask for a waking dream that would tell her clearly she should go.

Asking for a waking-dream symbol was one way Sandra had learned to listen to God. When she was very excited it was hard to listen. She asked to see a pair of praying hands. But so that she would know it was truly a sign from God, she wanted to see blue with it, the color of the light of the Mahanta that many people see with their inner vision. The color blue should be near or around the praying hands, Sandra decided.

The very next morning, as she turned on the television, Sandra saw her waking-dream symbol:

A woman was holding her hands in prayer fashion and was wearing a blue blouse.

The symbol was perfect. How could she question

> Asking for a waking-dream symbol was one way Sandra had learned to listen to God.

such clarity? Sandra went to the training. She has been following her heart ever since toward her goal.

Another instance of a waking dream was when I had decided to move to Portland, Oregon. My friends could not seem to find any logic in it, because they really didn't want me to leave. I knew I would miss them too, but I had fallen in love with Portland, and my job had ended. Since I liked Portland quite well and felt an inner nudge to move there, I decided I would go.

My mind began to nag at me. Was I being foolish? Was this really the right thing to do? I asked for a waking-dream symbol. If I saw a dozen fresh red roses the next day, I would move. How often does one see fresh roses?

The very next morning at my place of worship, there was something on the greeter's table I'd never seen before. Fresh flowers—and oh, how lovely they smelled. As I lifted my head from drinking in their aroma, I suddenly realized that here were my fresh red roses! And there were exactly one dozen.

I said to myself, "I guess I'm moving to Portland."

Over the next few months, while planning my move and finishing some work in Minnesota, I kept wondering again if it was really the right decision. I began to feel that I would dearly miss some of my friends there. But *I kept seeing dozens of fresh red roses.* (Later I learned that Portland is called the city of the roses, complete with a yearly Rose Festival.)

When I finally arrived in Oregon, it was November 1, and November there usually means rain every

> I asked for a waking-dream symbol. If I saw a dozen fresh red roses the next day, I would move.

day. It was an unusually rainy and very dark month. I was living in a very dark apartment and knew only one or two people. I felt very lonely and depressed, thinking perhaps I'd made a grave error by moving. Thank goodness I had another waking dream:

On Thanksgiving I went to a friend's home and walked in to find on her counter—that's right—a dozen fresh red roses.

I knew that for better or worse, I was home, and I'm very glad I stayed. There was much in Portland to learn, and it was a great place for me to begin new ventures. When it was time to leave Portland, I asked to see purple elephants if Holy Spirit really wanted me to move back to Minneapolis. Would you believe it? I saw purple elephants for months!

CAN WAKING DREAMS WARN US WHEN WE'RE OFF COURSE?

When we're not in the right place for us, Holy Spirit can warn us about it through waking dreams.

Many years ago I had a waking dream that steered me back to center. In the apartment building where I lived, the laundry room was always kept very clean. The hallways and outside walkways were always clear and clean as well. However, one week I saw something three times that made me think it was definitely a waking dream:

There were hangers hanging on the door in the laundry room and on the floor in the hallway. A few days later, they were still there and there were hangers on the sidewalk.

> When we're not in the right place for us, Holy Spirit can warn us about it through waking dreams.

I wondered, *What did it mean to see hangers everywhere?* I thought about what was going on in my life at the time. There were some personal issues holding me back.

I was too picky about time. I had to be exactly on time, and so did everyone else! I became very anxious when they weren't. And I felt like I was going to have a heart attack if I wasn't where I was supposed to be two minutes early!

Suddenly, I knew what the hangers meant. I had some hang-ups I needed to get rid of, and I knew just what they were. Laughing, I vowed to be less stiff and hung up about time. It was great to have the comic relief! God can be funny too.

Kerri asked the Mahanta for a warning in the form of a waking-dream symbol. She'd just been proposed to by a man named Tom. However, she'd been married before and was afraid of making a mistake again. Her divorce had been painful, and it had taken two years to recover. There was no way she wanted to go through that ever again!

While she was driving up a huge hill, approaching the top, Kerri asked for a waking-dream symbol to help her know what to do. As she drove over the top of the hill, she saw a wonderful sight.

A man was releasing white birds from a cage, and they were flying free! This meant to Kerri that she should feel free to marry Tom, and that their love was a pure love. After all, she did love him, and at that moment she knew there was really never any doubt in her heart. It had only been in her mind.

> Laughing, I vowed to be less stiff and hung up about time. It was great to have the comic relief! God can be funny too.

Someone else might have decided the birds meant, "This marriage is for the birds." However, Kerri knew how to interpret the answer for herself, and she knew she was just trying to find out what was already in her heart, what she already wanted as Soul. We all have the answers, as Soul, and we have inner guidance from the Mahanta if we ask. Waking dreams and dream symbols can reveal the path to our own inner temples.

The next waking dream she had was a nice surprise and a kind of wedding gift to her and her brand-new husband. *When they walked out of the church after their wedding ceremony, a van drove by with these words on its side: "Weddings and Happy Times."*

Tom and Kerri had both lived in that town for years before they even knew each other and had never seen such a van. Waking dreams are something Kerri pays a lot of attention to now. She finds they make her life much smoother.

> We all have the answers, as Soul, and we have inner guidance from the Mahanta if we ask.

WILL YOUR GREATEST HOPE COME TO PASS?

Waking dreams can help you prepare for the future by giving you markers along your route. Janet was looking for those markers.

Janet and her husband had decided to adopt a child, but they found out that adoption can be very difficult and often requires waiting a long time. Chinese babies, Janet had heard, were easier to adopt. She would try it. They began the process of adopting a baby from China. The trouble was there so many requirements, she was unsure they could fulfill them all. There was also a slowdown of babies arriving from China. Janet was beside herself with frustration. Nothing seemed to be working.

On Christmas Eve Janet and her husband went for a walk with their guests after dinner. They walked through the chilly streets of the small town in which they lived. Downtown was just a few blocks away, so they walked up to the main street, turned left, and immediately saw something they had never before seen.

An adoption agency had a sign that was lit up, even though it was closed. On the sign was a photo of a Chinese baby.

Janet and her husband knew this waking dream was their Christmas present, no matter how long it took for the baby to arrive.

The waiting seemed like an eternity to Janet, but God helped keep her spirits up through more waking dreams. For the next few months Janet kept seeing Chinese babies everywhere until she finally received her own precious gift from God!

Waking Dream Technique:
Life Is a Dream

1. Look for unusual happenings in your daily life. If you see them more than once, they may have some significance for you. Write them in your dream journal, right along with your dreams, and see if you can find a pattern.

2. If you would like an answer, write the question in your journal. Then ask for guidance and keep your eyes open for a symbol.

If you would like an answer, write the question in your journal. Then ask for guidance and keep your eyes open for a symbol.

3. You may set up your own symbol for ease of perception. Anything will do, but it helps if it is something you do not often see.

Enjoy all of your dreams as you would a garden filled with varied flowers, changing constantly with the seasons. They are a gift of love from God.

When I need some help with life and I don't remember my dreams, waking dreams become essential. They're my best counselors in times of confusion and a healing salve in times of sorrow.

If you'd like to learn more about all kinds of dreams, read the book *The Art of Spiritual Dreaming* by Harold Klemp. It will help you solve the wonderful mystery of dreams. Their secrets will unfold like a rosebud whose beauty is revealed in its fragrant petals.

And, enjoy all of your dreams as you would a garden filled with varied flowers, changing constantly with the seasons. They are a gift of love from God.

Glossary

Words set in SMALL CAPS are defined elsewhere in this glossary.

ARAHATA. *ah-rah-HAH-tah* An experienced and qualified teacher of ECKANKAR classes.

CHELA. *CHEE-lah* A spiritual student.

ECK. *EHK* The Life Force, the Holy Spirit, or Audible Life Current which sustains all life.

ECKANKAR. *EHK-ahn-kahr* Religion of the Light and Sound of God. Also known as the Ancient Science of SOUL TRAVEL. A truly spiritual religion for the individual in modern times. The teachings provide a framework for anyone to explore their own spiritual experiences. Established by Paul Twitchell, the modern-day founder, in 1965. The word means "Co-worker with God."

ECK MASTERS. Spiritual Masters who can assist and protect people in their spiritual studies and travels. The ECK Masters are from a long line of God-Realized SOULS who know the responsibility that goes with spiritual freedom.

GOD-REALIZATION. The state of God Consciousness. Complete and conscious awareness of God.

HU. *HYOO* The most ancient, secret name for God. The singing of the word HU is considered a love song to God. It can be sung aloud or silently to oneself.

INITIATION. Earned by a member of ECKANKAR through spiritual unfoldment and service to God. The initiation is a private ceremony in which the individual is linked to the Sound and Light of God.

LIVING ECK MASTER. The title of the spiritual leader of ECKANKAR. His duty is to lead SOULS back to God. The Living ECK Master can assist spiritual students physically as the Outer Master, in the dream state as the Dream Master, and in the spiritual worlds as the Inner Master. Sri Harold Klemp became the MAHANTA, the Living ECK Master in 1981.

MAHANTA. *mah-HAHN-tah*   A title to describe the highest state of God Consciousness on earth, often embodied in the LIVING ECK MASTER. He is the Living Word. An expression of the Spirit of God that is always with you.

PLANES.   The levels of existence, such as the Physical, Astral, Causal, Mental, Etheric, and Soul Planes.

SATSANG. *SAHT-sahng*   A class in which students of ECK study a monthly lesson from ECKANKAR.

SELF-REALIZATION.   SOUL recognition. The entering of Soul into the Soul Plane and there beholding Itself as pure Spirit. A state of seeing, knowing, and being.

THE SHARIYAT-KI-SUGMAD. *SHAH-ree-aht-kee-SOOG-mahd*   The sacred scriptures of ECKANKAR. The scriptures are comprised of twelve volumes in the spiritual worlds. The first two were transcribed from the inner PLANES by Paul Twitchell, modern-day founder of ECKANKAR.

SOUL.   The True Self. The inner, most sacred part of each person. Soul exists before birth and lives on after the death of the physical body. As a spark of God, Soul can see, know, and perceive all things. It is the creative center of Its own world.

SOUL TRAVEL.   The expansion of consciousness. The ability of SOUL to transcend the physical body and travel into the spiritual worlds of God. Soul Travel is taught only by the LIVING ECK MASTER. It helps people unfold spiritually and can provide proof of the existence of God and life after death.

SOUND AND LIGHT OF ECK.   The Holy Spirit. The two aspects through which God appears in the lower worlds. People can experience them by looking and listening within themselves and through SOUL TRAVEL.

SPIRITUAL EXERCISES OF ECK.   The daily practice of certain techniques to get us in touch with the Light and Sound of God.

SRI. *SREE*   A title of spiritual respect, similar to reverend or pastor, used for those who have attained the kingdom of God. In ECKANKAR, it is reserved for the MAHANTA, the LIVING ECK MASTER.

SUGMAD. *SOOG-mahd*   A sacred name for God. Sugmad is neither masculine nor feminine; It is the source of all life.

WAH Z. *WAH zee*   The spiritual name of Sri Harold Klemp. It means the Secret Doctrine. It is his name in the spiritual worlds.

For more explanations of Eckankar terms, see *A Cosmic Sea of Words: The ECKANKAR Lexicon* by Harold Klemp.

Notes

Chapter 1. Exploring the Spiritual World of Dreams

1. Harold Klemp, *How the Inner Master Works,* Mahanta Transcripts, Book 12 (Minneapolis: ECKANKAR, 1995), 215.
2. David Fontana, Ph.D., *Teach Yourself to Dream: A Practical Guide to Unleashing the Power of the Subconscious Mind* (San Francisco: Chronicle Books, 1997), 10.
3. Ibid., 38.
4. Harold Klemp, *The Spiritual Exercises of ECK,* 2d ed. (Minneapolis: ECKANKAR, 1993, 1997), 41.

Chapter 2. How to Interpret Your Dreams

1. Harold Klemp, *The Slow Burning Love of God*, Mahanta Transcripts, Book 13, 2d ed. (Minneapolis: ECKANKAR, 1996, 1997), 174.
2. Harold Klemp, *The Dream Master,* Mahanta Transcripts, Book 8, 2d ed. (Minneapolis: ECKANKAR, 1993, 1997), 32.
3. Donald W. Stewart and David Koulack, "The Function of Dreams in Adaptation to Stress Over Time," *Dreaming: Journal of the Association for the Study of Dreams,* Vol. 3, No. 4 (New York: Human Sciences Press, Inc., 1993).
4. Ernest Hartmann, "Making Connections in a Safe Place: Is Dreaming Psychotherapy?" *Dreaming: Journal of the Association for the Study of Dreams,* Vol. 5, No. 4 (New York: Human Sciences Press, Inc., 1995).

Chapter 3. Spiritual Problem Solving through Dreams

1. Klemp, *Spiritual Exercises of ECK,* 35.
2. The Editors of Time-Life Books, *Dreams and Dreaming: Mysteries of the Unknown* (Alexandria, Va.: Time-Life Books, 1990), 117.
3. Klemp, *Slow Burning Love of God,* 153–54.
4. Debbie Johnson, *Think Yourself Thin,* (New York: Hyperion, 1996*)*.

Chapter 4. The Miraculous Healing Power of Dreams

1. Klemp, *How the Inner Master Works,* 164.
2. Paul Twitchell, *The Flute of God* (Minneapolis: ECKANKAR, 1969).

192

3. Stewart and Koulack, "The Function of Dreams in Adaptation," 259.
4. Susan Sleeper-Smith, "The Dream as a Tool for Historical Research: Reexamining Life in Eighteenth-Century Virginia Through the Dreams of a Gentleman: William Byrd, II, 1674–1744," *Dreaming: Journal of the Association for the Study of Dreams,* Vol. 3, No. 1 (New York: Human Sciences Press, Inc., 1993).
5. Hartmann, "Making Connections in a Safe Place," 213.

Chapter 5. As Above, So Below

1. Klemp, *The Dream Master,* 185.
2. Stanley Krippner, Ph.D., and April Thompson, B.A., "A 10-Facet Model of Dreaming Applied to Dream Practices of Sixteen Native American Cultural Groups," *Dreaming: Journal of the Association for the Study of Dreams,* Vol. 6, No. 2 (New York: Human Sciences Press, Inc., 1996), 72.
3. Linda C. Anderson, *35 Golden Keys to Who You Are & Why You're Here* (Minneapolis: ECKANKAR, 1997).
4. Editors of Time-Life Books, *Dreams and Dreaming,* 99.
5. Harold Klemp, *What Is Spiritual Freedom?* Mahanta Transcripts, Book 11 (Minneapolis: ECKANKAR, 1995), 117.
6. J. Allen Boone, *Kinship with All Life* (New York, Harper & Row, 1954).
7. Klemp, *Slow Burning Love of God,* 179.

Chapter 6. Preparation, or Prophetic, Dreams

1. Klemp, *The Dream Master,* 128.
2. Editors of Time-Life Books, *Dreams and Dreaming,* 28.
3. Ibid., 131.
4. Ibid., 132.
5. Ibid., 42.
6. 2 Corinthians 12:2 Authorized (King James) Version.
7. Mary Carroll Moore, *How to Master Change in Your Life: Sixty-seven Ways to Handle Life's Toughest Moments* (Minneapolis: ECKANKAR, 1997).

Chapter 7. Past-Life Awareness in Dreams

1. Harold Klemp, *The Art of Spiritual Dreaming* (Minneapolis: ECKANKAR, 2000), 196.
2. Carlo D'Este, *Patton: A Genius for War* (New York: HarperCollins Publishers, 1995), 321.
3. Harold Klemp, A *Modern Prophet Answers Your Key Questions about Life,* (Minneapolis: ECKANKAR, 1998), 207–8.

Chapter 8. Recurring Dreams, Dreams of Intrusion, and Nightmares

1. Klemp, *The Dream Master,* 9.
2. Raymond E. Rainville, "The Role of Dreams in the Rehabilitation

of the Adventitiously Blind," *Dreaming: Journal of the Association for the Study of Dreams,* Vol. 4, No. 3 (New York: Human Sciences Press, Inc., 1994), 157.

3. Stewart and Koulack, "The Function of Dreams in Adaptation to Stress Over Time," 260.

Chapter 9. Dreams of Communication

1. Klemp, *Slow Burning Love of God,* 105.
2. John W. James and Frank Cherry, *The Grief Recovery Handbook: A Step-by-step Program for Moving Beyond Loss* (New York: Harper & Row Publishers, 1998), 148.

Chapter 10. Spiritual Experiences through Dreams

1. Klemp, *Slow Burning Love of God,* 174.
2. Wendy Doniger and Kelly Bulkley, "Why Study Dreams? A Religious Studies Perspective," *Dreaming: Journal of the Association for the Study of Dreams,* Vol. 3, No. 1 (New York: Human Sciences Press, Inc., 1993), 69.
3. Klemp, *Spiritual Exercises of ECK,* 5.
4. Editors of Time-Life Books, *Dreams and Dreaming,* 110.
5. Editors of Time-Life Books, *Dreams and Dreaming,* 113.
6. Editors of Time-Life Books, *Dreams and Dreaming,* 113.

Chapter 11. Worlds beyond the Dream World

1. Harold Klemp, *The Secret of Love,* Mahanta Transcripts, Book 14 (Minneapolis: ECKANKAR, 1996), 204.
2. Elisabeth Kübler-Ross, M.D., *Death Is of Vital Importance: On Life, Death and Life After Death* (Barrytown, N.Y.: Station Hill Press. Inc., 1995), 93.
3. Harold Klemp, *Journey of Soul,* Mahanta Transcripts, Book 1 (Minneapolis: ECKANKAR, 1998).

Chapter 12. Life Is But a Dream

1. Klemp, *How the Inner Master Works,* 217.
2. Traditional nursery rhyme.
3. Fontana, *Teach Yourself to Dream,* 17.

195

FOR FURTHER READING AND STUDY

How to Survive Spiritually in Our Times, Mahanta Transcripts, Book 16
Harold Klemp

A master storyteller, Harold Klemp weaves stories, tips, and techniques into the golden fabric of his talks.

They highlight the deeper truths within you, so you can apply them in your life *now*. He speaks right to Soul. It is that divine, eternal spark that you are. The survivor. Yet survival is only the starting point in your spiritual life. Harold Klemp also shows you how to gain in spiritual wealth. This book's a treasure.

Autobiography of a Modern Prophet
Harold Klemp

Master your true destiny. Learn how this man's journey to God illuminates the way for you too. Dare to explore the outer limits of the last great frontier, your spiritual worlds! The more you explore them, the sooner you come to discovering your true nature as an infinite, eternal spark of God. This book helps you get there! A good read.

The Art of Spiritual Dreaming
Harold Klemp

Dreams are a treasure. A gift from God. Harold Klemp shows how to find a dream's spiritual gold, and how to experience God's love. Get insights from the past and future, grow in confidence, and make decisions about career and finances. Do this from a unique perspective: by recognizing the spiritual nature of your dreams.

35 Golden Keys to Who You Are & Why You're Here
Linda C. Anderson

Discover thirty-five golden keys to mastering your spiritual destiny through the ancient teachings of Eckankar, Religion of the Light and Sound of God. The dramatic, true stories in this book equal anything found in the spiritual literature of today. Learn ways to immediately bring more love, peace, and purpose to your life.

Available at your local bookstore. If unavailable, call (952) 380-2222. Or write: ECKANKAR, Dept. BK39, P.O. Box 27300, Minneapolis, MN 55427 U.S.A.

THERE MAY BE AN
ECKANKAR STUDY GROUP NEAR YOU

Eckankar offers a variety of local and international activities for the spiritual seeker. With hundreds of study groups worldwide, Eckankar is near you! Many areas have Eckankar centers where you can browse through the books in a quiet, unpressured environment, talk with others who share an interest in this ancient teaching, and attend beginning discussion classes on how to gain the attributes of Soul: wisdom, power, love, and freedom.

Around the world, Eckankar study groups offer special one-day or weekend seminars on the basic teachings of Eckankar. For membership information, visit the Eckankar Web site (www.eckankar.org). For the location of the Eckankar center or study group nearest you, click on "Other Eckankar Web sites" for a listing of those areas with Web sites. You're also welcome to check your phone book under **ECKANKAR**; call **(952) 380-2222, Ext. BK39;** or write **ECKANKAR, Att: Information, BK39, P.O. Box 27300, Minneapolis, MN 55427 U.S.A.**

☐ Please send me information on the nearest Eckankar center or study group in my area.

☐ Please send me more information about membership in Eckankar, which includes a twelve-month spiritual study.

Please type or print clearly

Name _____
  first (given)   last (family)

Street_____ Apt. # _____

City _____ State/Prov. _____

ZIP/Postal Code _____ Country _____